LAND REGISTRATION

Global Practices and Lessons for India

LAND REGISTRATION

Global Practices and Lessons for India

By

B.K. Agarwal

PENTAGON PRESS LLP

Land Registration: Global Practices and Lessons for India
B.K. Agarwal

First Published in 2019

Copyright Reserved

ISBN 978-93-86618-86-3

All rights reserved. No part of this publication may be reproduced, stored in a retrieval system, or transmitted, in any form or by any means, electronic, mechanical, photocopying, recording, or otherwise, without first obtaining written permission of the copyright owner.

Disclaimer: The views and opinions expressed in the book are the individual assertion of the Author. The Publisher does not take any responsibility for the same in any manner whatsoever. The same shall solely be the responsibility of the Author.

Published by
PENTAGON PRESS LLP
206, Peacock Lane, Shahpur Jat,
New Delhi-110049
Phones: 011-64706243, 26491568
Telefax: 011-26490600
email: rajan@pentagonpress.in
website: www.pentagonpress.in

Printed at Aegean Offset Printers, Greater Noida, U.P.

"Land is the only thing in the world that amounts to anything, for it's the only thing in this world that lasts. It's the only thing worth working for, worth fighting for-worth dying for!"

— **Margaret Mitchell,**
Gone with the Wind

Contents

	Acknowledgements	ix
1.	**Introduction**	1
2.	**Basic Tenets of Land Registration**	6
	Deed Registration System	6
	Title Registration System	10
	Difference between Two Systems	13
	Registration Systems in Other Countries	14
3.	**Deed Registration: Study of Select Countries**	18
	Deed Registration in the USA	18
	Deed Registration in France	28
	Deed Registration in the Netherlands	33
4.	**Title Registration: Study of Select Countries**	40
	Title Registration in Australia	40
	Title Registration in England	50
	Title Registration in Germany	59
	'Mirror', 'Curtain' and 'Insurance' Principles	67
5.	**Title Registration: Theory and Practice**	70
6.	**Land Registration and Record-of-Rights in India**	76
	Registration of Deeds	77
	Record-of-Rights	80
	Law on Transfer of Property	88
	Strengths of Indian System	94
	Problems in the Present System	98

7.	**Relevance of Title Registration in India**	**102**
	Change-over to Title Registration Not Advisable	115
8.	**Recommendations for Improvement in Land Registration in India**	**120**
	Appendix A: **Analysis of Laws on Record-of-Rights in Select States**	**140**
	Record-of-Rights in Maharashtra	140
	Record-of-Rights in Karnataka	147
	Record-of-Rights in Punjab	152
	Record-of-Rights in West Bengal	159
	Bibliography	163
	Index	169

* * *

List of Boxes

Box 1:	Basic Tenets of Land Registration	11
Box 2:	Deed Registration in the USA	26
Box 3:	Deed Registration in France	32
Box 4:	Deed Registration in the Netherlands	37
Box 5:	Title Registration in Australia	47
Box 6:	Title Registration in England	59
Box 7:	Title Registration in Germany	67
Box 8:	Title Registration: Theory and Practice	74
Box 9:	Deed Registration in India	79
Box 10:	Analysis of Laws on Record of Rights in Select States	82
Box 11:	Record-of-Rights in India	87

Acknowledgements

Land Administration as a subject has fascinated me since I joined service but I could never devote enough time to study this subject in depth. About three years back I had irresistible urge to study this subject and applied for study leave of one year for this purpose. I am highly indebted to Shri M. Venkaiah Naidu, Honourable Vice President of India, who as Minister of Housing and Urban Poverty Alleviation granted me leave, making it possible for me to complete this work.

I am thankful to my IIT Roorkee classmate, Dr. Dinesh Kumar Likhi, Chairman and Managing Director of Mishra Dhatu Nigam Limited, who guided me to join IIM Lucknow to research on the subject of my interest. I express my sincere gratitude to Dr. Ajit Prasad, Director Indian Institute of Management, Lucknow who gave me opportunity to join his institute as Scholar-in-Residence during my study leave. Interactions with him and other faculty members have made significant contribution to this work.

I am very thankful to Prof. O.P. Mathur, Senior Fellow at the Institute of Social Sciences, New Delhi who has been constant source of inspiration and guidance during this work. He always made himself available whenever I requested him for any support.

I would like to thank Dr. O. C. Handa, a renowned scholar and an old friend for motivating me to get this work published.

My wife Sadhana Agarwal always stands beside me like a rock in all my endeavours. She has constantly inspired and motivated me to do my best during this work also. I am grateful to her for her moral and emotional support without which it would not have been possible to work for about two years on this study. I am also thankful to my children Animesh and Sonakshi for their support all along this work.

B.K. Agarwal

CHAPTER 1

Introduction

Land is an essential resource for any economic activity aimed at creation of material wealth in the world. The management of land resources, therefore, is considered an important component of the economic policies of a country. Land assumes a special significance in a developing country like India, which has recently started on the path of fast economic growth. Rapid economic growth in the last three decades or so has led to fast urbanization also. It is estimated that by 2051, 48 per cent of the total population will be living in cities. This demographic shift will generate a huge demand for housing and other urban infrastructure in the cities and adjoining rural areas. Further, to sustain a high growth rate of the economy, the country needs rapid industrial development and large investments in roads, railways, power, communication and similar infrastructure.

These requirements have opened a new opportunity for land owners to unlock the economic value of their land. However, transactions in land, which has suddenly become very valuable near urban centres, are giving rise to innumerable title disputes also. As per an estimate, a third of the cases pending in lower courts involve disputes over property. It is increasingly being felt that for faster development of the country, some way has to be found to reduce title disputes relating to land. This will attract investors, developers and financiers towards urbanization projects as risk towards title will be reduced.

Some experts believe that introduction of a system of 'conclusive title' in place of the existing system of 'presumptive title' on land is the only solution to solve the problems relating to land markets and land administration in India. As the Chairman of One-man Committee on Record-of-Rights in Land, D.C. Wadhwa in his report submitted to Planning Commission in 1989 recommended replacing the present system of presumptive rights over land with the system of conclusive title.[1] Swati Ramanathan has recommended the adoption of a system of state-guaranteed title registration in India because lack of clarity on records and rights impacts urban policies, urban planning and urban management.[2] The National Commission to Review the Working of the Constitution has also recommended that the state guarantee private and public land as one of the administrative reforms.[3]

In modern times most countries have a system of keeping a record of rights of the people over property and transfer thereof. However, there are wide variations in the features of such systems used by various countries because of historical reasons and also differences in the socio-economic conditions of each country. Generally, these systems are classified into two broad categories, viz., Deed Registration[4] and Title Registration. The Title Registration system is also sometimes referred to as 'System of Conclusive Title,' 'System of Guaranteed Title' or 'Torrens System.'

In the deed registration system, a written conveyance deed executed by the parties in respect of a transaction in property is registered with a registrar who does not go into the legal validity of the transaction. He only examines the formal requirements like identification of parties, their signatures and that of the witnesses, correctness of format of deed, etc. The record of registration is evidence of the transaction of property between the parties but is not conclusive proof of the transfer of title.

In the title registration system, when an application for transfer of ownership in a property is submitted to a registrar, unlike his counterpart in the deed registration system, he plays an active role and goes on to examine the legal validity of the transaction. He registers the transaction in a public register only if he is satisfied that the transferor has a clear title on the property and there is no legal hindrance in passing the title to the transferee. The title registration system provides a state guarantee of registered titles and generally an insurance fund to compensate owners whose interests are defeated due to any error made by the registrar. The cardinal principle is that the title register maintained by the government authority is everything, and a person whose title is recorded there has an indefeasible title over the land. If someone with a better claim comes forth later with evidence that the registration was in error, he does not get back the property but can receive damages paid out of a state insurance fund. In theoretical terms, he is protected by a liability rule, not a property rule.

Both these systems have a widespread following in the world and there are examples of successful land markets under both the systems. Among the top ten economies of the world, the United States of America, Japan, Italy, France, India and Brazil have the deed registration system; Germany and the United Kingdom have title registration; Canada follows both the systems and China is in the process of implementing the title registration system.

As has been mentioned earlier, some experts hold the view that India should change over to the title registration system to solve the problem of ever increasing land disputes. The Department of Land Resources, Government of India, also subscribes to this view and lists 'moving eventually towards guaranteed conclusive titles to immovable properties in the country'[5] as one of the objectives of the National Land Records Modernization Program (NLRMP) launched in 2008. While the Government of India is willing to provide financial support, the present system of land registration cannot be changed without the states taking the initiative in this regard. Under the scheme of division of subjects between the Union Government and the state governments under the Constitution of

India, 'maintenance of land records' and 'survey for revenue purposes and records of rights' are state subjects. Therefore, any law relating to registration of conclusive title has to be enacted by the states only. While considerable progress has been made by the states in implementation of other components of NLRMP, they have not done much towards introduction of conclusive titling.

Thus as the situation exists today, the Department of Land Resources, Government of India, has taken a policy decision to change-over to the system of conclusive title in the country but the states are not very confident in going for such a massive change in the legal system. Consequently, while this issue frequently finds mention in the reports of experts and the policies of the government, not much is happening on the ground.

A committee constituted by the Department of Land Resources, Government of India, to suggest a model and give a road map for implementation of land titling in the country has observed that 'a considerable amount of interest is generated towards titling among various states even though there is no clear direction as to where to begin and how to go about it.'[6] The observation of the committee describes the reasons for the slow action on the part of the states. To introduce the system of conclusive title, the states will require large-scale changes in the administrative and legal set-up relating to land records and land transactions. This effectively means doing away with a well established system of deed registration and maintenance of record-of-rights, which has been in use in the country for more than a century. As implementation of any such measure would be spread over a long time, results as to success or failure will be visible so late that it may not be possible to revert back. Therefore, a state normally will not go for it unless the problems with the present system are extremely acute and it is certain that switching over to the new system will solve them.

INTRODUCTION

In this context, there is a need for a comprehensive assessment of all the aspects relating to land registration in India and global practices in this regard. Without an objective evaluation of the real problems relating to land registration in India and the reasons behind them, a solution cannot be found. Global practices may provide important inputs for devising a solution but replicating those practices in the Indian set-up has to be examined carefully before adopting them.

The objective of this book is to examine all the issues relating to land registration in India and make evidence-based recommendations to improve the system. With this objective, the provisions of the Registration Act, 1908, the Transfer of Property Act, 1882 and state laws relating to maintenance of record-of-rights have been analysed to assess their strengths and weaknesses. Laws relating to record-of-rights of four states, viz., Maharashtra, Karnataka, Punjab and West Bengal have been examined in great detail and have been compared on the basis of some common parameters. Further an in-depth study of land registration systems in three deed registration countries, viz., the United States, France, the Netherlands and three title registration countries, viz., Australia, England and Germany has been done to know their systems and their relevance for India. Based on the analysis of the Indian system and global practices, some recommendations have been made to make improvements in the present system of land registration in India.

NOTES

1. (Wadhwa 1989)
2. (Ramanathan 2009) p. 22
3. (National Commission to Review the Working of the Constitution 2002)
4. It is called 'recordation system' in the United States.
5. (The National Land Records Modernization Programme, Guidelines, Technical Manuals and MIS 2008-09)
6. (land titling - A Road Map 2014)

CHAPTER 2

BASIC TENETS OF LAND REGISTRATION

In modern times almost every country has a system of recording the rights of people over property in some kind of public record. However, there are wide variations in the features of systems used by various countries for this purpose due to different socio-economic conditions and administrative history of each country. Generally, these systems are classified into two broad categories, viz., Deed Registration[1] and Title Registration. Among these two broad categories, there are many variations from country to country.

Deed Registration System

A deed registration system, in its simplest form[2], provides for execution of a written conveyance deed for transactions like sale, lease, gift, mortgage and registration with some public authority designated for this purpose. The record of registration is an evidence of the transaction between the parties and can be referred in case of any dispute later on. The designated authority, generally called a registrar, examines the formal requirements like identification of parties, signatures of the parties and witnesses, correctness of formats of deed, etc., and, if found in order, keeps a copy of the deed in his records arranged chronologically with time and date of presentation. The original deed is returned to the parties endorsing thereon the reference of registration.

Effect of Registration

In this system, the transaction is complete as soon as a deed is executed between the parties and registration is only for the purpose of maintaining records for future reference. In case of a dispute in the future, a registered deed gets priority over an unregistered one. In some countries like the United States of America and France, non-registration of a deed does not affect the legality of the transaction and has the only consequence of low priority in comparison with a registered deed. Some deed registration statutes, including that of India, however, provide that an unregistered deed will have no evidentiary value, making it mandatory for the parties to register a deed.

The record of registry is open to the public for inspection and getting copies if required. The registration of a deed is deemed to be a constructive notice to the whole of the world in respect of the transaction contained in the deed, meaning thereby that any person intending to deal with that property is supposed to know the existence of the registered transaction and the consequences thereof.

If a piece of land has been sold twice and only one transaction has been registered, the person claiming rights on the land through a registered deed will win in case of any dispute between the two claimants. The situation becomes complex when more than one deed has been registered in respect of the same property and a dispute arises between the two claimants. Deed registration statutes of different countries have different provisions for dealing with such a situation and on that basis are classified as race statute, notice statute, race-notice statute, hybrid statute or grace period statute.[3]

Registration Not Conclusive Proof of Title

The most important feature of the deed registration system is that registration is only evidence of a transaction and does not confirm transfer of title in favour of the transferee. The deed registration conforms to the rule of law *'Nemo dat quod non habet'*, literally meaning 'no one gives what he doesn't have'.[4] In the deed registration system, the actual transfer of title depends on many other factors that are not examined by the registrar at the time of registration. If the transferor does not have the right to transfer, the transferee will not acquire the title over the property in spite of the conveyance deed being duly registered. Any defect in the title of the transferor gets automatically transferred to the transferee. In the deed registration system, the parties are responsible for the validity of the transaction with the registrar acting only as the custodian of records.

Investigation of Title

Before purchasing a property, a person normally searches records of the registry to know the details of previous transactions in respect of that property to satisfy himself that the seller has undisputed title over the property. The general practice is to go through all the previous transfer deeds in respect of a property till a good 'root of title'[5] is found which may be an undisputed document like a government grant. If such a document is not found, the search is limited to a reasonable period in the past which is governed by local practices followed by the lawyers. In India, generally a search is made for the last 30 years. After the search, if an unbroken chain of legally valid transactions from the 'root of title' to the present owner is found, the intending purchaser would be satisfied with the title of the seller and may go ahead with the transaction.

In a basic deed registration system there is no uniform system of description of property under transfer. As per the convenience of the parties, a variety of markers may be used to identify the property like street name, geographical features, nearby permanent structures, adjacent properties, etc. In this system, a deed is registered with reference to the parties to the transaction and not with reference to a particular property. Many properties of different kinds and at different locations can be transacted through a single conveyance deed. Due to this reason searching the history of the title of a property is generally very cumbersome in a deed registration system. However some countries have made improvements in the system to overcome this problem.

Indexes to Facilitate Title Search

To facilitate search of deeds, the registrar maintains indexes as per provisions of the statute of that country. The simplest index is grantor-grantee index which lists the name of the grantors and grantees in alphabetical order.[6] Against their names are written brief particulars of the transaction.[7] Particulars to be mentioned in the index vary from country to country as per law and practices there.

Including reference to the copy of the deed preserved in the registry. However, it is difficult to trace the history of the title of a property from the grantor-grantee index because a previous owner of property under investigation may have executed many deeds in respect of his properties and all those deeds need to be examined for locating transactions in respect of the property under investigation.

To overcome this problem, some countries like India and a few states in the USA have provisions in the law for maintaining a tract-index in addition to a grantor-grantee index. In a tract-index, individual properties are arranged in a logical sequence with details of grantor, grantee and reference to the copy of the deed mentioned against them. However, an effective tract-index can be maintained only when there is a uniform system of identification of properties. Such a system exists in countries like India, France and the Netherlands where there is the practice of maintaining cadastre[8] on the basis of a cadastral survey. However, in countries like the USA where there is no tradition of making a cadastre, it is difficult to maintain tract-indexes.

Title Registration System

The other system is 'Registration of Title' which is prevalent in many countries like Australia, New Zealand, the United Kingdom, Germany and Canada. Though the title registration systems of various countries are substantially different from each other, certain common characteristics are found in all of them which distinguish them from the deed registration system. When an application for change of ownership or any other right in the property like lease, mortgage, etc., is submitted to a registrar he, unlike his counterpart in a deed registration system, plays an active role and goes on to examine the legal validity of the transaction in detail. He registers the transaction in a public register only if he is satisfied that the transferor has a clear title to transfer his right and there is no legal hindrance in passing the title to the transferee.

Mirror, Curtain and Insurance Principles

Ruoff[9] lays down 'mirror', 'curtain' and 'insurance' principles as defining features of a title registration system. The 'mirror' principle means that the register accurately reflects all the material facts relating to title; the 'curtain' principle implies that for ascertaining the title, no investigation beyond the register is necessary and the 'insurance' principle requires the state to guarantee the correctness of the register and compensate a bonafide claimant suffering a loss due an incorrect entry in the register. Hogg has classified those systems as registration of title systems where land is used as a unit of property, transactions are registered with reference to the land, registration of transaction is essential for its validity and registration acts in some degree as a warrantee of title of the person registered as owner.[10] The indemnity by the state has not been included by him as an essential characteristic of the title registration system.

> **Box 1: Basic Tenets of Land Registration**
>
> 1. A registered deed is only an evidence of transaction in land while an entry in the title register is conclusive proof of title.
> 2. In a deed registration system, the legal validity of a transaction is not examined but in a title registration system, registration is done after ascertaining the legal validity of the transaction.
> 3. Deed registration is with reference to the right holder while title registration is done with reference to a particular property.
> 4. Ruoff, Theodore B.F. in "An Englishman Looks at the Torrens System" has laid down 'mirror', 'curtain' and 'insurance' principles as defining features of a title registration system.
> 5. Among the top ten economies of the world, the USA, Japan, Italy, France, India and Brazil have deed registration systems, Germany and the U.K. have title registration, Canada follows both the systems and China is in the process of adopting title registration.
> 6. Due to their diverse features, land registration systems of various countries cannot be put into watertight compartments of 'Title Registration' and 'Deed Registration'. The Ontario Law Reform Commission says 'each is not a single system, but rather is composed of different alternatives and the combined alternatives form a continuum.'

Though the provisions of law in different countries vary, generally an entry in the register is considered sacrosanct even if it has been made due to some mistake on the part of the registrar or the parties to the transaction. A genuine right holder, who loses his rights in the property due to an incorrect entry in the register may claim monetary compensation for his loss but cannot get his property back. In countries like Australia, New Zealand and the United Kingdom, a fund has been created by the government to provide compensation in such cases. However, some countries like Germany, Austria, Israel, Malaysia, Sudan and Fiji do not have a government-sponsored fund for this purpose but an aggrieved person can claim compensation either from the government or from the defaulting party as per the general law of the land.

Registration Conclusive Proof of Title

Once an entry in the name of the transferee is made in the register, it is considered as conclusive proof of his title over the property. Armed with an entry in the register, at the time of the next transaction the transferee does not have to prove his title through a chain of previous transactions as is required in the case of deed registration. Also, transfer of title is complete only after an entry to this effect is made in the title register. An agreement between the parties to transfer the title is a precondition for registration but it has no value unless the transaction is registered. This legal position is in contrast to that in the deed registration system where the title is generally transferred at the time of execution of the conveyance deed. Registration of the deed is a subsequent act to give notice to the public, create evidence of the transaction and to assign priority against any competing transactions affecting the same property.

Registration with Reference to Particular Property

In a title registration system, the registration is always done with reference to a uniquely identified property and a separate folio is earmarked for each property in the register. To quote James Edward Hogg, who has done unparalleled work on comparative law, 'By title registration—or registration of title—is meant primarily a system under which the record is made of the title to some particular land as vested in some particular person for the time being.'[11] Though, the methodology of identification, description of property in the records and fixation of boundaries varies from country to country, registration with reference to a particular property is the central feature of title registration in all the countries.

Difference between Two Systems

Sometimes, the title registration is put in contrast to the deed registration system as if these are the only two mutually exclusive choices before a country. In practice however the features in the property registration systems used by various countries are so diverse that it is difficult to put them into watertight compartments. Various writers have used different criteria to distinguish registration systems existing in various countries from each other. Norman[12] has used the terminology of positive and negative systems of land registration. 'On this terminology, a "positive" system is one in which the state warrants that the rights shown on the register are valid and effective according to their terms. ...In a "negative" system, registration does not confer or guarantee the title, with the result that purchasers must examine the deeds and draw their own conclusions.'[13] The Scottish Law Commission describes a positive system as bijural, because two legal principles operate in this system and a negative system as monojural.[14]

Deed registration in Scotland (before Scotland switched to title registration in 1975) and South Africa have long been recognised having almost all the characteristics of title registration. The deed registration system of the Netherlands is often labelled as semi title registration system.[15] The title registration system of Germany does not have a provision for state guarantee which is laid down as an essential principle of title registration by Ruoff. Deed registration in the USA, in conjunction with title insurance by private companies, provides similar indemnity to the purchaser as available in the title registration systems of England and Australia. In India, after registration of deeds, entries are made in the record-of-rights against uniquely identified properties which is actually a feature of the title registration system.

Therefore, it is not correct to describe these two classes of registration systems as mutually exclusive. 'The two classes shade off into each other and it is a matter of some difficulty to distinguish with complete accuracy between registration of title and registration of deeds.'[16] The Ontario Law Reform Commission says 'Each is not a single system, but rather is composed of different alternatives, and the combined alternatives form a continuum. The major variable in this continuum is the extent of the affirmation made by the province of the existence and ownership of interests.'[17]

If private conveyancing, as it existed in England before the Land Registration Act, 1925, is placed at the extreme left of this continuum, the Torrens system of Australia would find a place at the extreme right. The deed registration system, as it exists in India, the USA and many other countries, would get a place closer to the left end and the registration system of England would be placed somewhere in the middle while Germany's place would be closer to the right end.

Registration Systems in Other Countries

Though a country would choose a system of land registration mostly on the basis of internal factors, international experience does sometimes play a role in building an opinion in the government in favour or against a system. Therefore, while assessing the suitability of title registration[18] for India, a factual review of prevalence of deed registration and title registration in other countries is useful to ensure objectivity in the decision-making process.

James Edward Hogg, who made a comprehensive study of land registration systems in the British Empire as early as in 1918, observed that:

> 'In the British Empire and in the United States, taken together and separately, the territories in which registration of deeds (as an adjunct to conveyance of deed) is the only system are far more numerous than those which have introduced a system of registration of title. Even in the latter a system of deed registration also prevails side by side with registration of title, except in the case of a small minority. ... Thus roughly one-

third of the Anglo-American world favours registration of title, and two-thirds favour conveyance by deed registration.'[19]

The situation has not changed substantially since Hogg made this observation. There are very few examples of countries switching over from a well-established deed registration system to title registration in the 20th or 21st century. The USA has rather seen a reverse trend in this regard. While 19 states introduced title registration between 1895 and 1917, only eight are presently using this system, that too as an option to landowners alongside a deed registration system. Among these states also, only Minnesota, Massachusetts and Hawaii use this system in all the counties alongside deed registration. In the other five, viz., Colorado, Georgia, North Carolina, Ohio and Washington, it exists only in a few counties each.

In Canada, some provinces have a deed registration system while some others use title registration. In Europe, title registration and deed registration are used in almost equal measure. To mention a few countries, Austria, Denmark, the United Kingdom, Finland, Germany, Poland, Portugal, Spain, Sweden and Switzerland have title registration, while Belgium, France, Greece, Italy, Luxembourg and the Netherlands use the deed registration system.[20] Latin American countries predominantly follow the deed registration system. The title registration system was adopted in Brazil in 1890 but is not used much today. Title registration has also failed in other parts of Latin America.[21] In Asia, while Japan and India have deed registration, Malaysia, Indonesia, the Philippines, and China have adopted the title registration system. Hong Kong had enacted the Land Title Ordinance in 2004 but implementation has been kept in abeyance due to objections on many provisions by the Bills Committee of the Legislative Council.[22]

Among the top ten economies of the world, the USA, Japan, Italy, France, India and Brazil have deed registration systems; Germany and the United Kingdom have title registration; Canada follows both systems and China is in the process of implementing a title registration system. Thus, both the systems have a widespread following in the world and there are examples of very successful land markets under both the systems.

NOTES

1. It is called 'recordation system' in the United States of America.
2. There are wide variations in the system of deed registration from country to country. In this chapter features of basic deed registration system are described.
3. (Simpson 1976) p. 96
4. 'Nemo dat quod non habet', is a legal rule, sometimes called the *nemo dat* rule, which states that the purchase of a property from someone who has no ownership right on it denies the purchaser also any ownership right.
5. Root of title refers to basic title deed which proves that the vendor has the right to sell the property.
6. The party transferring title in property is called grantor and the recipient is called grantee
7. Particulars to be mentioned in the index vary from country to country as per law and practices there.
8. A Cadastre is normally a parcel based, and up-to-date land information system containing a record of interests in land (*e.g.* rights, restrictions and responsibilities). It usually includes a geometric description of land parcels linked to other records describing the nature of the interests, the ownership or control of those interests, and often the value of the parcel and its improvements. (Definition of cadastre by the International Federation of Surveyors)
9. (Ruoff 1952) as cited in (Stein 1983) p. 269
10. (Hogg, *Registration of Title to Land Throughout the Empire* 1920) p. 2
11. (Hogg, *Registration of Title to Land Throughout the Empire* 1920) p. 1
12. (Norman 1965) as cited in (Simpson 1976) p. 21
13. (O'Connor, *Deferred and Immediate Indefeasibility: Bijural Ambiguity in Registered Land Title Systems* 2009) p. 195
14. (*Scottish Law Commission* 2004) p. 3.
15. (Louwman, *Advantages and Disadvantages of a Merger Organisation: The Case of the Kadaster- Netherlands* 2017) p. 5
16. (Hogg, *Registration of Title to Land Throughout the Empire* 1920) p. 2
17. (*Law Reform Commission Ontario* 1971) p. 19
18. 'Title registration', 'conclusive title' and 'guaranteed conclusive title' broadly mean the same and have been used interchangeably in this book.

19. (Hogg, *Registration of Title to Land* 1918) p. 52
20. *(Real Property Law and Procedure in the European Union* 2005) p. 32
21. Alejandro M. Garro 1989 as cited in (McCormack 1992) p. 63
22. *(The Land Registry, The Government of Hong Kong Special Administrative Region)*

CHAPTER 3

Deed Registration: Study of Select Countries

One of the objectives of this book is to analyse the experience of other countries in respect of deed registration and title registration. In this chapter, the deed registration in some select countries has been examined. The basic features of the deed registration system have been described in the previous chapter. However, there are substantial variations in the legal provisions of various countries following this system. For the purpose of this study, three countries, viz., the USA, France and the Netherlands have been selected as they provide a wide spectrum of variations in deed registration laws. The USA does not maintain a cadastre but has the unique feature of title insurance by private insurance companies. In France, cadastre is an important feature of the registration system but is maintained by an authority other than the registrar. In the Netherlands, the functions of cadastre and deed registration have been entrusted to a single authority. There are many other differences in the law and procedures of these countries which will be discussed in detail in this chapter.

Deed Registration in the USA

In the USA, the subject of laws on real property has not been delegated to the Federal Government and therefore the states have their own system of keeping real property records. Most of the states follow the deed registration system which is called 'recording system' there. All the states have their own recording laws which may have substantial differences in the procedures regarding presentation of documents in the registry and keeping the registered documents for future references. Though recording of the deeds is done as per the statute enacted by the state, the registry is entirely operated by the county government or municipal government with no intervention by the state government in day-to-day functioning. The head of the registry is normally a political appointee. Usually, deeds related to sale, mortgage, long term lease, trust, easement rights and other such instruments affecting rights in the property are required to be registered.

History of Deed Registration in the USA

Property law in the USA is heavily influenced by English law. However, registration of conveyance was introduced in the American colonies very early in contrast to England where no registration could be introduced till 1925. The first recording Act was enacted in Massachusetts in 1640 which introduced deed registration in the American continent with the objective of 'avoiding all fraudulent conveyances and that every man may know what estate or interest other men may have in any houses, lands or other hereditaments they are to deal in.'[1] Under this Act, however, the sole function of the registry was to create an index of legal conveyances with the minimum required details. A copy of the conveyance deed was not retained by the registry at that time. Later, New York, founded by Dutch immigrants, adopted the recording system prevalent in the Netherlands at that time. Under this system, not only was a register created but copies of conveyance deeds were also preserved in the registry. This system was gradually adopted in all the colonies of the continent.

Investigation of Title

In the deed registration system, a title search is the most important process to ensure that the buyer[2] of a property gets what is being promised to him and there is no third party claim resulting in loss of ownership or monetary loss to the buyer later. A buyer is protected against any previous transaction if he did not have actual and constructive notice of it. Recording of a transaction is considered a constructive notice against the whole world including any subsequent buyer. Therefore, for the buyer of a property it is essential to search the records of the registry to ensure that the seller has a good title and has not sold the property or created any other interest in favour of someone else prior to the proposed transfer.

A prospective buyer normally engages an attorney to examine the records and advise him whether, after the proposed transaction a good title will be transferred to him. This process is called title search which normally involves two professionals; an abstractor and a qualified attorney. An abstractor searches through all the records of the registry and compiles details of all the transactions related to the property proposed to be transferred in the form of an 'abstract'. On the basis of this abstract, the attorney gives his professional opinion on the legality of the title of the seller and any risk of future litigation.

Ideally, all the previous deeds in respect of the property back to the initial grant from the sovereign should be examined. However, it is not practically possible and if done may be very expensive for the buyer who has to bear the cost of search of the title. As per the accepted practice of the conveyancing bar, titles are examined only to a certain length of time in the past, usually sixty years.[3] Some states have enacted marketable title acts to provide a legal footing to this practice of examining deeds up to a limited period in the past.

Indexes Maintained by the Registry

The ease and accuracy of a title search is greatly dependent upon the indexes maintained in the registry. In the eastern part of the USA (the original 13 colonies[4]), the index is based on the names of the grantor[5] and grantee called 'grantor-grantee index'.

The names of the grantors are arranged alphabetically in the index with details like name of grantee, document reference, description of property, etc., mentioned against them. Normally, there is a separate index in which the names of the grantees are arranged alphabetically with name and other relevant information mentioned against each grantee. As transactions are not indexed with reference to individual properties, it is a tedious job to trace all the transactions relating to a particular property through the granter-grantee index and is amenable to errors also.

It is much easier to search title through a tract-index because all the transactions related to a property can be found at one place. The western states require or at least allow maintenance of parcel-based or tract-based indexes. The property is identified on a map which is mostly a map maintained by the tax authorities and the deed registration number and other details are linked to this geographic location. However, even in those states where the law provides for tract-based index, most of the counties still maintain granter-grantee indexes only because of relative ease in maintaining it in comparison to a tract-index. Another issue in maintaining a tract based index is that the USA does not have a uniform system of identification of geographic location of a property. Different states and counties use various kinds of maps for this purpose. This also is an impediment to the maintenance of tract-based indexes in the USA. The result is that the tract indexes are not provided for in most of the states and wherever they are provided for; they are usually limited to a few populous urban counties.[6]

Marketable Title Acts

Enactment of Marketable Title Acts is one of the many reforms taken up in the USA to improve the operation of the deed registration system. There may be certain interests of ancient origin on a property which have not been asserted in the recent past and therefore it is difficult for a prospective buyer to discover them. Some ancient interests may not appear on the record of the registry at all and therefore would not be discovered even when all the deeds relating back to the initial grant from the sovereign are examined. 'The advantages of marketable title acts are that they eliminate all defects, including those that do not appear on the records, against which there is otherwise no protection aside from title insurance.[7] Many times, such interests may not have a real significance but by remaining on the records they affect the marketability of the property. The Marketable Title Act aims to eliminate such old defects from the title of property by putting a time limit on their continuation if not asserted as per provisions of the Act.

The first such Act was enacted in Iowa in 1919 but the enactment of the Marketable Record Title Act, 1945 by Michigan began the trend of making such laws in other states. Since then, about a third of the states have enacted this type of legislation. The Uniform Law Commission of the USA circulated a Model Marketable Act in 1990 to help the states in drafting their law on this subject.[8] As per this Act, any interest that is not on the record of the previous thirty years is automatically extinguished, with some limited exceptions. One such exception is possession of the property. The right of a person in possession of the property is not extinguished even though there is nothing on the records of the previous thirty years. A right holder, however, can preserve his interest by recording it in the registry within the prescribed time under the Act. Once recorded, interest will be preserved for the next thirty years after which it would need to be recorded again to get validity for the following thirty years.

With the Marketable Title Act in place, an owner is assured of a good defect-free title if nothing adverse appears in the records of the last thirty years. A buyer also needs to examine title records of only 30 years prior to the date of buying to be reasonably sure that he would not face a legal problem afterwards. Though the enactment of marketable title acts has generally been hailed as a good reform, some experts criticize it on the ground that it violates permanent protection built into the recording process. It puts a genuine right holder in the danger of losing his rights if he fails to record it every thirty years due to ignorance or otherwise.

Failed Experiment with Title Registration

The success of title registration in Australia created enthusiasm among scholars and administrators in the USA to also adopt the new system which appeared at least theoretically to be a complete solution to all the problems related to land disputes. Illinois was the first state to adopt title registration in 1895 in Cook County (Chicago). This adoption was triggered by the great fire of Chicago in 1871 in which all the records of the registry were destroyed. As there were no records of deeds to investigate one's title over the land, it was found appropriate to introduce registration of title which, as a concept, did not require previous records once title was proved before the registrar and recorded in the register. Ironically however, in Illinois, title registration was not extended beyond Cook County which also fully abandoned it in 1992.

Following Illinois, some other states also adopted this system. From 1895 to 1917, nineteen states enacted title registration laws. However, none of the American States made title registration compulsory. It was introduced as an optional system of registration alongside deed registration with the expectation that landowners would come forward to register their titles to take advantage of a secured title under the title registration system. It was gradually realised that this expectation was ill-placed and people preferred deed registration supported by title investigation by attorneys and title insurance by private companies.

Present Status of Title Registration

In spite of 19 states introducing title registration, it never got wide acceptability in the USA. In some states, registration caught some momentum in the beginning which declined with the passage of time. Many states have repealed the titles registration laws, New

York being the latest to discontinue with title registration in 2000. At present, only eight states are using the title registration system. Among them only Minnesota, Massachusetts and Hawaii follow this system in all the counties alongside deed registration. In the other five states, viz., Colorado, Georgia, North Carolina, Ohio and Washington, it exists only in a few counties each. Thus the USA has tried title registration extensively, only to reject it finally.

Order of Judicial Court for First Registration

In the USA (in the areas where title registration is still existing) for registration of his title for the first time, a landowner has to approach a judicial court for an order establishing his clear title. The court refers the case to an official examiner on whose report a final decision is made by the court. If the court is satisfied with the claim of the landowner, a certificate of title is issued. The title is then registered in the registry on the basis of the certificate issued by the court. This procedure is much more cumbersome than that in England and Australia where decision on the application is made by the registrar only, without intervention of the judicial courts. However, it is simpler than the other option of 'quiet title action'[9] available in the USA to settle a disputed title. So, in the USA, title registration has been 'used largely as an alternative to quiet title actions to clear known or perceived defects in title.'[10] Actually, the original law enacted by Illinois in 1895 had the provision of issue of certificate of title by the registrar only, without intervention of judicial courts. However, this provision was held unconstitutional by the Supreme Court of Illinois on the ground that conferment of judicial power on an administrative officer was contrary to the doctrine of separation of judicial and executive power on which the United States Constitution is based.[11] Consequently, a new Act had to be brought in 1897 which provided for judicial determination of title before registration. Subsequently, other states also made similar provisions in their laws.

Title Insurance

Title insurance is an innovative practice introduced in the USA in the second half of the nineteenth century to provide security of title to a buyer of a property. The groundwork for the model and the concept of title insurance was laid by the famous Benjamin Franklin. At the time of purchase of a property, a buyer normally buys a title insurance policy from one of the many private title insurance companies working in the USA. Generally, a bank or any other lending agency does not finance a purchase of property without the buyer taking a title insurance policy. This policy insures him against any future loss due to any defect in the title of the seller or any undetected encumbrance on the property. The insurance company undertakes to compensate the insured for the actual loss along with the legal expenses to defend his case. Normally banks that finance the property also take a similar policy to protect their loan in case of any dispute on the property. In the case of these policies, a one-time premium is payable at the time of purchase and the insurance coverage lasts as long as the property is owned by the insured person.

Records Maintained by Insurance Agencies

Some insurance agencies maintain what they call 'title plants' which are actually tract-based registers of title. As has been discussed in the previous sections, in most of the states in the USA, only grantor-grantee indexes are maintained. The title registration companies acquire details of land transactions from the office of the registrar and rearrange them as per geographical location of the property. They keep these records updated all the time by taking necessary abstracts from the office of the registrar every day. On the basis of the records maintained in the 'title plants,' staff of the insurance agency is able to search the title history quickly and with a high degree of accuracy.

> **Box 2: Deed Registration in the USA**
>
> 1. Deed Registration, called 'Recording System' there, is the predominant system used for keeping records of property in the USA.
> 2. About a century ago, alongside deed registration, title registration was introduced in 19 states as an optional system. However, title registration never got wide acceptability in the USA.
> 3. All except eight states have now repealed title registration laws. Only Minnesota, Massachusetts and Hawaii have this system in all the counties (alongside deed registration) while in Colorado, Georgia, North Carolina, Ohio and Washington, it exists only in a few counties each.
> 4. The enactment of the Marketable Title Acts is one of the many reforms taken up in the USA to improve the operation of the deed registration system.
> 5. Title insurance by private insurance companies was introduced in the USA in the second half of the nineteenth century to provide security of title to the buyer of a property. The groundwork for the model and concept of title insurance was laid by the famous Benjamin Franklin.
> 6. Title insurance in the USA performs the same function as is performed by government-sponsored indemnity or insurance fund in Australia and England.

Risk Elimination vs. Risk Assumption

Title insurance is a unique product which differs in many respects from other types of insurance. While other types of insurance indemnify an insured against future events, title insurance policies generally insure owners and lenders against the losses caused by title problems that have their source in past events. Due to this reason it is possible to reduce the risk of the insurance agency by searching the past title records and identify a potential source of defect in the title of the seller. Before issue of a title insurance policy for a property, the insurance company searches the records to detect any defect in title or encumbrance on the property. If any such thing is found, the insurance company requires the buyer and the seller to take necessary steps to remedy the defect. Thus, title insurance works on the model of 'risk elimination' rather than a model of 'risk assumption' in other types of insurances.

Title Insurance makes up for Deficiencies in the System

Title insurance in the USA is popular because of deficiencies in the records maintained by the deed registries. The insurance agencies duplicate the records of the registries in a manner that makes searching of the title easier and more effective. Interestingly, title insurance is popular even in those states where title registration is available. It is so because under the title registration system, it is cumbersome to claim compensation from the government. A person has to go for long-drawn out litigation before he gets his claim from the government. On the contrary, an insurance claim is paid to the insured very quickly without asking many questions. Thus, title insurance in the USA performs the same function as is performed by government-sponsored indemnity or insurance funds in Australia and England.

Criticism of Title Insurance

Though title insurance is providing a very important service, it has been facing severe criticism also. As title insurance works on the model of risk elimination, a very small part of the premium collected by insurance companies goes into paying claims. Because of this title insurance, companies earn huge profits every year. To curb the tendency of the insurance companies, the insurance premium is regulated by the government in some states. Iowa has banned title insurance by private companies. There, insurance is provided under the Title Guarantee Program run by the Iowa Finance Authority which costs a fraction of what is charged by insurance companies in other states.

Deed Registration in France

The requirement of registration of land transactions was first introduced in France in 1798 which was later abolished by the French Civil Code of 1804. However, registration was reintroduced by the Land Registration Act, 1855[12] and since then France has been following the deed registration system in contrast to title registration in other European countries like Germany, Austria and the United Kingdom. The deed registration system of France has been improved significantly by linking it to the cadastre. The present form of the deed registration system in France has been established after major reforms were introduced in 1955.[13]

The authority responsible for registration of deeds and preserving the records is the mortgage registry (*conservation des hypothèques*) headed by a mortgage registrar. Since 2012, the name of this office has been changed to Land Registry Services (*services de la publicité foncière*). To ensure enforceability against third parties, it is compulsory to register the transactions and legal facts affecting the property like sale, gift, easement, long-term leases, court orders, government orders, death of a person, etc. The orders of the court affecting rights in the property are required to be registered before they can be enforced against third parties.[14] French property law follows the principle of *Numerus clauses* and limits the interests that can be held in land.[15]

Effect of Registration

In France, transfer of property is completed as soon as a deed is executed by the parties. Registration is required only for enforceability against third parties.[16] As is the practice in most of the deed registration systems, the registrar only looks in to the formalities of registration like proper execution, identification of parties, payment of registration fee, etc., without examining validity of rights involved in the transaction. Therefore, the registration does not correct any defect in the title of the grantee. It only assigns a priority to the transaction to resolve any dispute when more than one conflicting transactions related to the same land are executed. French law can be classified as a race statute because in case of two competing registered deeds in respect of the same property, priority is decided solely on the basis of date of registration, irrespective of the date of execution.[17] Registration also has the effect of giving notice to the general public about the transaction and as per law no unregistered transaction can be enforced against a third party.

Process of Registration

In a sale transaction in France, the first step is the signing of a preliminary agreement by the seller and the buyer which includes sale price, all the rights of the third parties like easements and mortgages and all other conditions precedent to the sale. This contract does not require a certification by the notary. Normally a part of the sale consideration is exchanged at this stage. After this, the notary engaged by the parties proceeds to complete the formalities for registration of transaction in the land registry. In France, registration can be applied only on the basis of the deed duly certified by a notary. A document for registration is required to be presented in the registry within three months in ordinary cases and within six months if transfer is because of the death of the owner.

Role of Notary

The notary completes verification of title, mortgages, easement rights, planning restrictions, pre-emption rights, etc., before preparing the sale deed to be signed by the parties and witnesses in his presence. He normally traces the chain of previous owners for the last thirty years.[18] It sometimes takes several months to complete this process. The institution of notary in France is considered very reliable which offers sufficient security of title to the buyer. A notary is responsible for searching the status of the property in the records of the land registry to ensure that no fact goes undetected which may affect the title of the buyer after the sale. In the case of any lapse on this account, he can be sued by the parties to compensate any loss caused because of his negligence in this respect.

Provisional Registration

When two parties have struck a deal and are in the process of completing the formalities for the execution of a deed and its registration, there is a possibility of registration of another deed concerning the same property by some other person through an act of fraud or misrepresentation. In such a situation, the rights of the person who has already struck a deal with the owner may be adversely affected. To prevent such cases, French law provides for provisional registration even before all the formalities for registration are complete. Provisional registration reserves the rank of the transaction in the register and can be done on the basis of a preliminary contract between the seller and the buyer. The parties can submit the required documents for final registration within a period of three years. Provisional registration in French law is similar to registration of priority notice in Germany.

Standardized Formats for Conveyance Deeds

The decree of 1955 provides that a deed should be written as per standardized formats as prescribed in the law.[19] These standard formats have been prescribed by the government in consultation with the council of notaries. These standardized formats have a simplified interpretation of rights contained in a deed. On registration, one copy of the deed is bound in the publication register (*register des publication*) and the original is returned to the applicant with the date of filing and reference number of the registry.

Registry Liable for Incorrect Information

The records of the land registry office are accessible to the public. On the application of a person who shows his legitimate interest in a property, the registry is obliged to provide all the information relating to the ownership and other rights on that property. The registry is also responsible for any loss suffered by any person due to incomplete or incorrect information provided by the registry.[20]

Real Estate File

The real estate file (*fichier immobilier*) was started in 1955 in France with the purpose of providing a document where the rights in a property are mentioned against uniquely identified property. This is a major reform in the deed registration system which establishes a correspondence between the deed registry and the cadastre. Legally speaking, it is only a supplementary register or index but now it has become the most important record relating to rights in the property. The introduction of the real estate file has greatly improved the operation of the deed registration system in France. In this file, details of all the right holders and transactions relating to a property are recorded. Each parcel of land is described as per its description in the related cadastre to ensure the unique identification of each property. Therefore, in the real estate file the status of ownership and other rights on a particular parcel of land can be ascertained easily. On the one hand, it compiles information about ownership and other rights in respect of a particular property in one folio and on the other it ensures perfect correspondence of land registry records with the cadastre. In its content, the real estate file of France is almost similar to the Land Register (*Grundbuch*) of Germany but differs in the legal force of the entries. While an entry in the *Grundbuch* is conclusive proof of title, the real estate file only records evidence of a transaction.

Cadastre

France like most of the countries of continental Europe has a long history of maintaining cadastre[21] for the purpose of assessment and collection of tax on land. Napoleon I, in 1807, had instituted the cadastre in France and most of the southern and western parts of continental Europe.[22] In France, the reference administrative unit for preparing cadastral records is the commune which is roughly equivalent to a municipal corporation. The cadastral mapping is done on a scale varying from 1:5000 to 1:500 with the most common scale in rural areas being 1:2000 and in urban areas 1:1000. Apart from the cadastral map, a set of documents is also part of cadastre which has textual information in respect of each land parcel marked on the map. The information contained in these documents includes cadastral identification number, reference of real estate file maintained by the land registry, area, address of the property, details of the owner and record of successive transaction in the property.[23] It is open to the public and anyone can inspect it and request for copies. Cadastre is maintained by the General Tax Directorate of France.

Box 3: Deed Registration in France

1. In France, deed registration and cadastre (similar to record-of-rights in India) are dealt with by different agencies as in India.
2. The notary is responsible for examining past transactions in land and giving correct advice to the parties. He also verifies the execution of the deed by the parties. This verification is done by the registrar in India.
3. A notary can be sued by parties for any loss due to his negligence or incorrect advice.
4. A person can claim damages from the government for loss due to any incorrect information given by the registry.
5. Introduction of 'Real Estate File' in the deed registry in 1955 has brought about a major improvement in the deed registration system.
6. A deed has to be written as per standardized formats which have been prescribed by the government in consultation with the council of notaries.

Cadastre and Real Estate File in Conformity

The cadastre and real estate file though maintained by different authorities are kept in correspondence by regular exchange of information. The parcel reference of a property in the real file is compulsorily based on the cadastre and ownership information in the cadastre is entirely sourced from the real estate file. However, a cadastre may not always show up-to-date status of the ownership and other rights on the property, the authentic source of which is the real estate file only.

Determination of Property Boundaries

The quality of cadastral maps is not uniform throughout the country and many a time the cadastral map is inadequate to determine the precise boundaries between land parcels. In the case of a dispute on this account, the owners normally hire a qualified private surveyor to fix the boundaries. If the owners agree among themselves on the disputed boundaries, they sign an agreement to this effect; otherwise they have an option to settle the matter in the civil court. The services of private surveyors are also taken to prepare a new plan in case of the sale of a part of the land parcel. This plan is checked by the local cadastral authority before filing with the land registry along with the sale deed.

Deed Registration in the Netherlands

The Netherlands, like France, also has a well-established system of making cadastre along with the deed registration. Cadastre was introduced here by Napoleon after its annexation to France. Survey of land was begun in 1812 which was continued by King William I even after the fall of Napoleon. A country-wide fiscal cadastre was completed in 1832 (only province Limburg was finished in 1838).[24] In 1811, it was decided that all the deeds of transfer and of mortgage should be recorded with the national tax department to facilitate levy of transfer taxes. On the basis of these recorded documents changes were made in the cadastre also. In 1824 recording of deeds in the registry was made compulsory.

The deed registration system of the Netherlands is largely based on French law in this respect. However, over the years, many modifications have been introduced in the system to provide better security of title and better service to the people. Due to these modifications, the Dutch system is sometimes referred to as 'semi title system'.[25] Instead of going into the procedural details of the Dutch system which is mostly similar to the deed system of France, it would be more useful to study the reforms made by the Netherlands in the system. In next few paragraphs such reforms and their implication will be described.

Single Agency for Deed Registration and Cadastre

In 1927, a single officer was made responsible for the register of deeds (called 'public register'), as well as the cadastre. In every deed registration system, an index of registered deeds is created to facilitate investigation into the title of the owner of property. In France, this index is called the real estate file. In the Netherlands also indexes were earlier prepared by the registrar. However, since 1927, the preparation of a separate index by the registrar was discontinued and it was decided to use the cadastral register as an index for the public register. This ensured complete correspondence between the cadastre and public registers. In 1994, the task of registration and cadastre was transferred to Cadastre, Land Registry and Mapping Agency (also called Kadaster) which is an independent public body constituted by a special law, the 'Cadastre Organization Act'.[26]

Registration Mandatory for Transfer of Title

Normally in the deed registration system, title is transferred when a valid contract is executed between the parties and consideration is exchanged. The registration of deed is required only for its enforceability against third parties. However, in the Netherlands, title is not transferred until the deed is registered in the registry. Due to this provision, unlike in the deed registration systems of France, registration in the Netherlands has a constitutive effect, but registration of deed still does not guarantee the title. In other words, the registration of deed is one of the necessary but not the only conditions of the transfer of title.[27]

Security of Title of a Bonafide Buyer

In a conventional deed registration system, registration of a defective deed does not transfer ownership. Because of this legal position, a buyer has to investigate all the previous deeds to ensure that there is no defect in any of them which may create an uncertainty regarding his title. In the Netherlands, the deed registration law has been modified to give protection to a third party who has acquired property in good faith relying on the last deed registered in respect of that property. The new Civil Code in 1992 provided that 'if a sellers (sic.) right is defective and the buyer has sold to a third person who is in good faith, the third person keeps the property.'[28] This provision, with certain limitations, provides a good security of title to a bonafide transferee relying on the records of the registry which is normally available in the title registration systems only. Because of this provision a notary in the Netherlands normally investigates only the last deed instead of screening all the deeds till a good root of title is obtained which is the practice in France and the USA.[29]

Liability of Government for Loss to True Owner of Property

In the Netherlands, while security of title is provided to a person who buys a property in good faith on the basis of the last deed registered, the true owner who loses his right because of this law is also not left unprotected. As per the Civil Code (Art. 3:30), the government is liable in cases where a loss is caused to a true owner, without any fault of his, because of the protection provided to the third party. Similarly The Cadastral Agency is also liable for its mistakes causing loss to a person with regard to the maintenance of the cadastre and public registers.[30]

Registrar Plays Active Role

In the deed registration system, the registrar plays a passive role and does not investigate the legal validity of the contents of a deed. He is mandated to register any deed presented to him if it fulfils the formal procedural and legal requirements. It is for the parties to investigate the validity of the title before entering into a transaction. In the Netherlands, without changing this legal position substantially, the registrar has been authorized to inform the parties if he thinks that the transferor does not have a valid title or is not authorised to transfer the property.[31] In such cases, the registrar first informs the notary, who in most of the cases withdraws the deed submitted by him on behalf of his client. In the unlikely event of parties insisting on registration of such a deed, the registrar is obliged to register it. However, the registrar can put an objection at the time of giving effect to this transaction in the cadastre.

Notice to Parties before Entry into Cadastre

Though the cadastre is used as an index to the public register, changes in it are not incorporated solely on the basis of registration of a deed in the public register. A notice is sent to all the affected parties regarding intended changes in the cadastre giving them an opportunity to submit an objection.[32] On the basis of the objections, or his own observation regarding a defect in the deed, the registrar (who is incidentally the same authority who registered the deed but acting in a different capacity) may decide not to enter the name of the transferee in the cadastre. In such cases, the affected parties may approach the civil courts for appropriate remedy. This provision of examination of title before making an entry in the cadastre has increased the reliability of records in comparison to normal deed registration systems. 'Thus in fact the Dutch system for recording deeds in public registers displays some similarities with that of a registration of titles in which the registrar rejects an application when the supposed transferor has no right to do so.'[33]

Box 4: Deed Registration in the Netherlands

1. Deed registration and cadastre both are dealt with by an independent public body called 'Kadaster', constituted by a special law.
2. The Cadastral register (similar to record-of-rights in India) is used as an index for deed registration also. Preparation of separate indexes by the registry has been discontinued.
3. Unlike France, in the Netherlands title is not transferred until deed is registered. This is almost similar to the legal position in India.
4. The Registrar has been authorised to examine the validity of the transaction and inform parties about any infirmity noticed by him. However, the parties can go for registration ignoring his advice.
5. The deed registration law has been modified to give protection to a person who has acquired property in good faith relying on the last deed registered in respect of that property.
6. Due to many improvements made in the traditional deed registration system, the Dutch system is often described as a 'semi title system'.
7. In 1950, the Dutch Parliament rejected a proposal to introduce title registration because deed registration was functioning well in practice.

The Netherlands, in spite of having a deed registration system, is 'supporting an active land market, with an acceptable level of security'.[34] After inheriting a conventional deed registration system from France, the Netherlands has constantly introduced new procedures and practices to improve the system to provide better service to the people. In 1950, the Dutch parliament, while declining a proposal to introduce the title registration system, held the opinion that the 'system functioned so well in practice that the law did not need to be amended extensively.'[35]

As discussed in the previous paragraphs, three developed countries have been continuing with the deed registration systems. They have made certain improvements in the system based on their specific requirements. The USA has title insurance, France has introduced Real Estate File and the Netherlands has made specific provisions in the law providing security of title to a bonafide buyer.

NOTES

1. (Simpson 1976) p. 96
2. Reference to buyer also includes reference to a mortgagee, lessee and person acquiring any such right in the property for valuable consideration.
3. (Barnett 1967) p. 91
4. The term 'Original Thirteen Colonies' refers to a group of British colonies on the east coast of North America founded in the 17th and 18th centuries that declared independence in 1776 and formed the United States of America.
5. The party who transfers title in property is called grantor and the recipient is called grantee.
6. (Barnett 1967) p. 51
7. (Barnett 1967) p. 85
8. (Uniform Law Commission, the United States 1990)
9. In the USA 'quiet title action' is a lawsuit brought in a judicial court in order to establish a party's title to the property against anyone and everyone, and thus "quiet" any challenges or claims to the title. It is similar to 'suite for declaration' under the Specific Relief Act in India.
10. (Justin T Holl 2010) p. 24
11. (Simpson 1976) p. 87
12. (Vliet 2017) p. 23
13. (Decree No. 55-22 of 4 January 1955 on the reform of registration of land 1955) (Decree No. 55-22 of 4 January 1955 on the reform of registration of land 1955) (*Décret n°55-22 du 4 janvier 1955 portant réforme de la publicité foncière*)
14. (Decree No. 55-22 of 4 January 1955 on the reform of registration of land 1955) Art. 28
15. (Glok 2016) p. 4
16. (Glok 2016) p. 2
17. (Decree No. 55-22 of 4 January 1955 on the reform of registration of land 1955) Art. 30
18. (Glok 2016) p. 32

19. (Decree No. 55-22 of 4 January 1955 on the reform of registration of land 1955)
20. (French Civil Code) (French Civil Code) Art. 2449, 2450
21. A Cadastre is normally a parcel based, and up-to-date land information system containing a record of interests in land (rights, restrictions and responsibilities). It usually includes a geometric description of land parcels linked to other records describing the nature of the interests, the ownership or control of those interests and often the value of the parcel and its improvements (Definition of cadastre by the International Federation of Surveyors)
22. (J. Zevenbergen 2002) p. 28
23. (Gil 2002)
24. (Willem Jan Wakker 2003) p. 4
25. (Louwman 2017) p. 5
26. (Willem Jan Wakker 2003) p. 5
27. (Kadaster, Netherlands) p. 2
28. (Louwman, *The Integration of the Cadastre and Public Registers in the Netherlands*)
29. (Kadaster, Netherlands) p. 1
30. (Hendrik Ploeger 2016) p. 22
31. (Hendrik Ploeger 2016) p. 14
32. (Louwman, *The Integration of the Cadastre and Public Registers in the Netherlands*)
33. (Kadaster, Netherlands) Land Transaction and Registration Process in the Netherlands, p. 2
34. (J. Zevenbergen 2002), p. 135
35. (J. Zevenbergen 2002) p. 139

CHAPTER 4

Title Registration: Study of Select Countries

Many countries in the world follow the title registration system to record rights in property. The basic features of title registration have been described in the second chapter. However, there are substantial differences in the laws of different countries. On the basis of the differences in their laws, Dowson and Sheppard have classified title registration countries in five groups, viz., the English Group, the Torrens Group, the German Group, the Swiss Group and the Ottoman Group.[1] For the purpose of this study, three countries, namely, Australia, England and Germany which belong to different groups, have been selected for a detailed examination of their laws and practices.

Title Registration in Australia

Any discussion on land title registration always begins with Australia because it was here that a pioneering effort was made to introduce a registration system which became a model throughout the world. In 1858, a system of registering ownership and other interests in land was introduced in South Australia on the initiative of Sir Robert Richard Torrens. This system was so different from the prevailing system in Australia and England at that time that it came to be known as the Torrens system after its inventor. It was introduced in South Australia through the enactment of the Real Property Act, 1858. Later, similar enactments were made in other states of Australia also.[2] The enactments of all the states follow the same pattern with minor differences. Before discussing these enactments it will be helpful to know the history of land ownership in Australia.

History of Land Ownership in Australia

The colonization of Australia began on 26 January 1788 with the arrival of the 'First Fleet' led by Captain Arthur Phillip at Port Jackson in New South Wales and under the instructions from the British Crown established a British colony there. To exclude the native residents altogether from the land, in 1835 a the Governor of New South Wales issued a proclamation that the land belonged to no one prior to the British Crown taking over its possession. Further, a proclamation was issued by the British Government also to declare that all persons occupying land without the authority of the British Crown will be considered trespassers. These two proclamations had the effect of abolishing all the rights and titles of original inhabitants over the land. From now onwards, a valid title could be acquired only through a crown grant under the Crown Lands Act, 1861.

These proclamations immensely simplified the titles in Australia because from now onwards the title of every parcel of land could very easily be traced from the crown grant which was in the form of a comparatively recent legal document. Additionally, measurements and clear boundaries of each parcel were available in the document containing the Crown grant. This situation is in contrast to a country like India where the ownership history of a piece of land may go up to thousands of years without any written document about the title of the first owner. This system was also followed in all the colonies set up after New South Wales. Australia as a country came into existence in 1901 when six British colonies decided to form a federation with the capital at Canberra.[3]

Private Conveyancing

In the initial years of colonization, the English system of private conveyancing was practised in Australia which did not require any kind of registration. Transfer of land from an owner to another was done through a contract between them which sometimes was reduced to writing in the form of a conveyance deed and sometimes the ownership was transferred just by an endorsement on the back of a document containing the Crown grant. A landowner was not required to approach any authority for transferring his land and consequently no public record of such transfers was available. When a land changed many hands, the only proof of ownership of land was a chain of successive conveyance deeds or other such documents preserved by the current landowner.[4]

Deed Registration

The registration of deeds was first introduced in New South Wales through a Governor's proclamation in 1817 which was followed by the enactment of the Registration of Deeds Act, 1925. Gradually, all the states enacted laws regarding registration of deeds.[5] It is interesting to note that despite being British colonies all the states in Australia brought in statutes relating to registration of deeds while, at that time, no such registration system existed in England except for a very rudimentary deed registration system in the counties of Middlesex and Sussex. The registering authority maintained name-based vendors and buyers indexes. There was no practice of maintaining land parcel-wise indexes. It was very difficult to find the status of a particular parcel of land from the records of the registrar and a transferee had to depend mainly on the conveyance deeds retained by the vendor for verifying the correctness of his title over land.

Introduction of Title Registration

Title registration was first introduced in South Australia by Sir Robert Richard Torrens through the enactment of the Real Property Act, 1858. The other states followed this move with their own enactments. Since then, these enactments have gone through many amendments, some of them having been altogether replaced by new enactments. The enactments of all the states follow the same pattern with minor differences. As the minor differences are not relevant to the purpose of this study, the common features of these laws will be discussed in this section. A reference to the specific provision in an enactment of a state may be given to illustrate a point assuming that a similar provision exists in other states also.

The Torrens System introduced in South Australia was a major deviation from the law and practices prevailing at that time. This system provided for maintenance of record of title with reference to individual parcels of land in contrast to maintenance of record with reference to seller and buyer in the earlier deed registration system. At the time of registration of a transaction in land, a separate folio in the register of title was created for each parcel under transfer with all the details of ownership and other rights mentioned therein. This was a major reform because earlier there was no system of keeping a separate record of ownership for each parcel of land. Under the earlier enactments regarding registration of deeds, the registering authorities kept a copy of the transfer deed which might affect more than one parcel of land. A buyer had to sift through many sale deeds to ascertain whether the seller had a good title over a particular parcel of land and that there were no other interests like mortgage, easements, etc. on it.

Process of Title Registration

After introduction of the title registration system, all the subsequent Crown grants were directly registered in the title register and further transactions in them was allowed through registration of title only. This made the implementation of the new law very easy because the registrar did not encounter the problem of investigation of title at the time of first registration. It was easy to operate this system later also because 'a title good at the time of grant could easily be kept good by efficient record backed by law'.[6]

It is the duty of every person acquiring any right over a land to get it registered with the registering authority failing which his right is not recognized under the law. Every state has created a central registry where all the transactions in respect of land are recorded in a register. This register contains all the details of ownership and other rights like leases, easements and mortgages. Under the Torrens System the registering authority examines the validity of the transaction on the basis of all the relevant documents before allowing registration in the name of the transferee. The transferee acquires a valid title only after the registration. Thus, under the Torrens system one does not register the title but gets title by registration.

The registrar provides a certificate of title in respect of each parcel of land registered with him which is conclusive evidence of his title over that land. The certificate of title describes all the facts regarding that property on the date of issue of title which includes lot number and plan number of land, details of registered proprietor and a description of all the interests that benefit or burden the land such as mortgages, caveats, leases, easements, covenants, etc. In this system, once a title over a land is registered, it cannot be challenged by any one on the basis of any infirmity in the title of any of the previous owners. In this system the registering authority does not play a passive role of registering whatever deed is presented before it but it is mandated to play an active role by examining the previous records, going into the correctness of the present title of the transferor and hearing the objections of any third party before registering the transfer of title. Because of this active role mandated by law, the registration of title in this system is considered as conclusive evidence of title over a piece of land.

Indefeasibility of Registered Title

The principle of indefeasibility of registered title has been very clearly laid down in the Torrens legislation of all the states in Australia. The object of the Real Property Act, 1886 of South Australia is mentioned as 'to secure indefeasibility of title to all registered proprietors, except in certain cases specified in this Act'. The Act further provides that, 'a certificate of title must be accepted in legal proceedings as conclusive evidence of title to land'.[7] The title of a registered proprietor is not affected by any error or omission in the process of registration. A registered title also prevails against any interest, encumbrances, liens, etc., which are not specifically notified on the certificate of title.[8] An intending buyer is not required to investigate into the validity of the title of a registered proprietor or his predecessor. He can buy the land relying on the entry in the register.[9] A bonafide buyer for value is fully protected against any defect in the title of the seller. Australian laws provide protection to a buyer against any unregistered interest in land irrespective of whether he had notice of such interests or not.

Indefeasibility of the Title of Volunteers

While Torrens laws provide protection to a purchaser for value in no uncertain terms, the protection to the volunteer, i.e. a donee or a successor of a deceased who has not paid for the acquisition of property is somewhat ambiguous. The statutes in Queensland and Northern Territory provide for full protection to the title of volunteer but in other states this issue has been subject to varied legal interpretations. Therefore, in Australia, indefeasibility of title of volunteers is not equivalent to that of a purchaser for value and depends on the interpretation of facts and law in each particular case.

Exceptions to Indefeasibility of Torrens Title

There are certain exceptions to the assurance of indefeasibility which mainly relate to acts of fraud, forgery, misrepresentation of facts, misdescription of property, etc. In such cases the aggrieved party can use appropriate legal remedies as available in case of unregistered properties. The title of the person involved in fraud or forgery is not protected by law even if the title is duly registered. However, if the disputed property has been bought bonafide by another person from a person responsible for fraud or forgery, the title of the new buyer is protected. For example, if 'B' has acquired land through fraud or forgery causing loss to 'A', the latter can lodge a criminal or civil case in an appropriate court to get 'B' prosecuted, claim compensation from him or get his land back by cancellation of certificate of title issued to 'B'. However if, before initiation of legal proceedings, 'C' has bonafide purchased land from 'B' without being aware of such illegality, his title will not be affected and he will have full protection of principle of indefeasibility.[10] Thus, in case of fraud or forgery, only the actual defaulter can be sued or prosecuted and title of all the subsequent owners remains indefeasible. This is a major deviation from English Common Law where any defect in the title of an owner makes the titles of all the subsequent owners defective.

Indemnity by the State

To protect persons deprived of their rights on the property either due to fraud, forgery and misdescription of property by another person or due to any omission or error on the part of the authorities, there are provisions to compensate his monetary loss. The Real Property Act, 1886 (South Australia) provides for an Assurance Fund from which such aggrieved persons can be compensated.[11] Other states also have similar provision in the law. This Fund is primarily financed by an assurance levy charged on registration of every title. There is also a provision for grants from the government in case the money in the Assurance Fund falls short of claims.

In South Australia, Western Australia, Tasmania and Australian Capital Territory an aggrieved person gets compensation from the Assurance Fund only if it is not possible to recover his loss from the defaulter through court proceedings. The aggrieved person has to file a case in the appropriate court for the compensation against the persons at fault. If compensation cannot be recovered from the defaulter due to death, bankruptcy or any other reason, the court may order its payment from the Assurance Fund. However, if loss has been caused due to any omission or error on the part of the authorities, the aggrieved person has the option to file a claim directly with the registrar also.

> **Box 5: Title Registration in Australia**
>
> 1. Title registration law was first enacted in South Australia in 1858 by Sir Robert Richard Torrens.
> 2. In Australia, all the rights of original inhabitants were abolished. So the title of every parcel of land could very easily be traced from the Crown grant. This situation was in contrast to a country like India where the ownership history of a piece of land may go up to thousands of years without any written document about the title of the first owner.
> 3. Title registration was made compulsory only for land granted by the British Crown after the enactment of the title registration law. Land granted earlier could continue to be transacted under the deed registration system. The implementation of the new system was simplified due to this provision.
> 4. Due to this, the dual system of title registration and deed registration exists even today in most of the states of Australia.
> 5. A registered title is indefeasible except in the case of fraud, forgery, etc. A bona fide buyer for value is fully protected against any defect in the title of the seller.
> 6. A person deprived of his property due to incorrect registration is paid compensation by the government from the Assurance Fund. However, in most cases, an aggrieved person has to first approach a civil court for recovery of compensation from the defaulter. Compensation from the Assurance Fund is paid as a last resort.
> 7. In Australia, no Cadastre is maintained as is done in India, France, Germany and the Netherlands. Stand-alone maps of properties are prepared at the time of registration to be attached with the title register.

Restrictions on Indemnity

Initially, all the state statutes relating to title registration provided unconditional indemnity to a person suffering loss due to fraud and errors in the registration process. However, there is now a trend to restrict right to indemnity in Australia. Many states have amended their statutes to deny or restrict indemnity in those cases where the loss is caused, wholly or partly, by fraud or negligence on the part of the claimant.[12] So now a person is not assured of full compensation in the case of loss. He has to prove his innocence and also that he took all due care to prevent such loss.

Maps and Boundaries of Land

In Australia, registration not only certifies the existing interests in land but also its boundaries. There was a system of accurately surveying each parcel of land at the time of Crown grant. As there was no system of preparing topographical or cadastral maps of the whole area, a stand-alone map (called plan) of parcels under the grant was prepared with reference to nearby landmarks. This map was attached with the land grant to be used for fixing the boundaries later in case of any dispute. The plan attached with the Crown grant was made part of the title register also. If a part of the land is to be transferred in a transaction, a new plan, prepared by a qualified surveyor, has to be submitted along with the application for registration of transfer of title. Thus, the title registration system in Australia is based on the survey of individual parcels of land which is done with great accuracy to enable demarcation of boundaries any time later. However, there is no linkage of these survey plans with cadastral or topographical maps of a larger administrative division.

Deed Registration still Continues

It is noteworthy that the registration of title was made compulsory only for the lands that were granted by the Crown after the enactment of the title registration law. It was optional for the owners of the lands granted earlier to bring their land under title registration or continue to transact them under the deed registration system. A majority of such owners did not come forward for registration of their title and therefore the dual systems of title registration and deed registration continues to exist even today in most of the states of Australia. Also, only land granted to private persons was registered under this system. Land which was not granted or land being used by government agencies was not entered in the title register. A landowner can convert his old system land[13] to the Torrens system by filing an application with the registrar along with proof of his title and a survey plan prepared by a qualified surveyor. The registrar examines all the documents and gives notice to all persons who might be interested in the property. After examination of documents and hearing the parties, if he is satisfied that there is no defect in the title, registration is done and a certificate of title is issued to the applicant.

Even after a century of operation of the Torrens system, large areas of land still remain outside this system. 'This was due mainly to a cumbersome application process that imposed onerous evidentiary requirements, coupled with ultra-conservative policies of administration and lack of staff in the Registrar's office.'[14] Simpson has cited Ruoff who, on Australian procedure of first registration, has commented that 'In the usual course of events there are lengthy advertisements, a multitude of inquiries, vexatious requisitions, costly surveys, and a meticulous and pessimistic scrutiny of every deed and event on the title covering very long periods, perhaps 100 years or even longer'.[15]

Qualified and Limited Titles

To encourage conversion of old titles into Torrens titles, all the states have taken steps to simplify the process of registration in case of old system land. The State of Victoria, by an amendment in law in 1986, allowed qualified titles to be issued on the basis of certification of a solicitor regarding soundness of a title.[16] Now all the states follow the procedure of issue of qualified and limited title without going for a detailed investigation. In most of the cases, the title is issued on the application of the landowners without any detailed investigation by the registrar with a qualification that the title is based on 'old system' documents that have not been investigated and that the title is subject to any subsisting interest under the old system. If no dispute arises, this qualification and warning is removed after a particular period of time which varies from state to state.[17]

If a new plan of survey is not filed along with an application to register old system land, the registrar issues a 'limited title' which means that actual boundaries have not been compared with the boundaries as shown in the earlier deeds of transfer and therefore the boundaries are not guaranteed by the registrar. This limitation can be removed when a plan of survey is filed and no discrepancy is found in the actual boundaries and boundaries described in the earlier deeds.

Title Registration in England

The United Kingdom has four regions, viz., England, Wales, Scotland and Northern Ireland. England and Wales use the same land law which is commonly described as English land law. Scotland and Northern Ireland have their own laws relating to land. This study covers only English land law as applicable to England and Wales.

Earlier System of Conveyancing in England

Till the time title registration was introduced in England, land was transferred through private conveyancing with the assistance of lawyers. The parties to the transaction retained conveyance deeds as proof of title and there was no system of keeping any record of such transactions with any public authority.

Anyone desirous of buying a particular property would engage a lawyer to investigate into the title of the seller and any encumbrances or equitable interests associated with the land. The seller would present all the previous conveyance deeds retained by him which would be carefully examined by the lawyer of the buyer to rule out any defect in title and also to find out any encumbrances or equitable interests on the property. If no defect is detected in the title of the seller, a deed would be executed to complete the sale. On completion of the sale all the previous deeds would be handed over by the seller to the buyer who would retain them as proof of his title.

Introduction of Registration of Title

The system of registration of title was first introduced in England in 1862. It was not introduced to replace the deed registration system but to fill a void because property transactions were not recorded anywhere at that time. Before the enactment of the Land Registration Act, 1862, there was no system of registration of either title or deed in England with the exception of deed registries established in the counties of Yorkshire and Middlesex in the early eighteenth century. The only record of such transactions was in the form of conveyance deeds preserved by the parties themselves without any involvement of a public authority.

Failure of Early Title Registration Legislations

Based on the report of a Royal Commission submitted in 1857, the Land Registration Act, 1862 was enacted 'to give certainty to the title to real estate, and to facilitate the proof thereof, and also to render the dealing with land more simple and economical.'[18] The registration of title was voluntary under the Land Registration Act. It was expected that landowners will come forward for registration as it would give certainty to their title and make future transactions more simple and economical. The response of the landowners was far from encouraging as only 547 applications were received and only 349 properties could be registered from 1862 to 1869.[19]

Another Royal Commission was appointed to go into the reasons for the failure of this Act and make suitable recommendations. On the basis of the report of this Commission submitted in 1870, a new statute, the Land Transfer Act, 1875, was enacted 'to make further provision for simplification of title to land and for facilitating the transfer of land'.[20] This Act however was even less successful, as only 113 titles were registered in the next ten years up to 1885.[21] To remedy this situation, the Land Transfer Act, 1897 was enacted which had a provision that a County Council can make registration compulsory in any area within its jurisdiction. Under this provision, however, registration was made compulsory only in the County of London in 1902, leaving it purely voluntary in the rest of England.

In spite of three enactments and the best efforts of the government for about 40 years to establish a land title registration system, the situation was far from satisfactory. So yet another Royal Commission was appointed in 1908 to consider the defects in the 1897 Act. This Commission in its report submitted in 1911 recommended that for the registration to be successful there was a need to substantially reform the law relating to real property. It also recommended that the task of proving title before the Registrar should be simplified as much as possible.

Reforms in English Property Law

A committee of the House was set up in 1919 which "agreed unanimously that the existing law of real property is archaic and unnecessarily complicated (and) that no great improvement in the existing systems of transfer of land, whether registered or unregistered, can be effected until the law of Real Property has been radically simplified".[22] With this background, sweeping changes in the laws relating to real property in England were made in 1925 by abolishing and amending many laws applicable at that time. The following legislations were enacted covering the whole field of real property law:[23]

   1. The Law of Property Act deals with estates, trusts, co-ownership of land, contracts and conveyances, formalities, leases and tenancies in outline, and burdens such as

mortgages, easements and covenants, and also important definitions.
2. The Settled Land Act deals with landed estates.
3. The Trustee Act regulates the powers and duties of trustees.
4. The Land Charges Act regulates the registration of burdens against titles which are unregistered
5. The Administration of Estates Act lays down the system of intestate succession and the procedure for handling estates of the deceased.
6. The Land Registration Act provides for registration of titles to the land itself.

The new Land Registration Act, 1925 repealed the Land Transfer Acts of 1875 and 1897. The actual registration of title in England began with this Act only. In the new Act, the power to make registration compulsory was taken from the County Council and given to the Central Government. The compulsory registration was gradually extended to different parts of the country. Finally, in 1990 the whole of England and Wales was brought under compulsory registration.'[24] Thus, the task of making registration compulsory in the whole of England and Wales could be accomplished 65 years after the Land Registration Act, 1925 came into force.

Review of Land Registration Act, 1925

In 1996, the Law Commission and HM Land Registry of the UK began a joint programme to update and reform the law relating to land registration. The recommendations of the Law Commission were published in 'Land Registration for the Twenty-First Century: A Conveyancing Revolution'. On the basis of this report, the Land Registration Act, 2002 was enacted repealing the Land Registration Act of 1925. The explanatory notes to the new Act published by the Government of the UK give some insight into the state of title registration since 1925.

Describing the basic structure of LRA 1925, it reads: 'That legislation [LRA 1925] provides an improved machinery of conveyancing rather than changing the underlying law, which applies to both unregistered and registered conveyancing. Its principles and definitions have sometimes been found obscure and confusing, and its language not easy for even professional users'.[25] These observations show that in spite of the best efforts, LRA 1925 could not establish an ideal title registration regime in England.

Registration of Title under Land Registration Act, 2002

The objective of the Act as mentioned in the preamble is 'to make provision about land registration; and for connected purposes'. This is in contrast to The Real Property Act, 1886 of South Australia which announces right in the beginning 'The objects of this Act are to simplify the title to land and to facilitate dealing therewith, and to secure indefeasibility of title to all registered proprietors, except in certain cases specified in this Act.' Under the Land Registration Act, 2002, the registration of title is compulsory only at the time of transfer of an unregistered estate by way of sale, gift, inheritance, etc. There is no compulsion for the present owner to get his land registered until he decides to transfer it to someone else.

Process of Registration

Land registration in England is conducted by the Land Registry which is an independent body set up under the Land Registration Act, 2002. In every district there is a District Land Registry headed by a registrar. The District Land Registrar is legally qualified, generally a solicitor, and is assisted by a number of staff technically qualified in law and mapping. Under English law, multiple estates can be created over the same physical piece of land. For example, if a piece of land is owned by a person on freehold basis, it will form a freehold estate over that land. If the owner leases out this land to someone for more than 7 years, the lessee will hold a leasehold estate on the same land. Further, on every sublease of this land a new estate will be created. Every estate can be registered as a separate title in the registry. In the title register, land is described mostly through postal address, supplemented by a title plan drawn from the large scale Ordnance survey map. The scale of these maps which is too small to fix the precise boundaries.

Conclusiveness of Registered Title

Towards conclusiveness to the registered title, the Act provides that a legal estate shall be deemed to be vested in the registered proprietor even if it would not otherwise vest in him.[26] This means that if a person is registered as the proprietor of an estate in a land, his title cannot be questioned on the basis of any defect in the transfer.

This normally should mean that if a person is registered as the proprietor of an estate in a land, his title cannot be questioned on the basis of any defect in the transfer. Thus, even if a person is registered as proprietor on the strength of a defective title of the Seller or forged transfer, the legal estate nevertheless should vest in him by virtue of registration. However, this conclusiveness provided in English law is not as robust as in Australian law.

Making an important improvement over the 1925 Act, a registered proprietor, under LRA 2002, has been conferred with unlimited power to dispose of an estate if there is no entry of charge, notice or restriction in the register. The title of the buyer is protected even if any limitation to the power of the proprietor is discovered later. The provisions regarding conclusiveness of the registered title, unlimited powers of the registered proprietor to dispose of the land [sec. 23] and protection of the title of the buyer [secs. 26 and 29] present a scheme which appears to protect the title of the present proprietor who has taken the estate for valuable consideration even if there was some defect in the title or limitation on the powers of the previous proprietor.

However, conclusiveness provided in English law is not so

straight. In some cases, courts have accepted the challenge to the ownership of a registered title holder and have decided that due to operation of the Act, he may hold 'legal estate' but the beneficial owner of the estate is that person who, in the opinion of the court, was deprived of his ownership due to wrong registration in the name of the present proprietor. Thus, the provision of the Land Registration Act to provide indefeasible title to the registered proprietor has been diluted by court decisions in England. As the law stands today, a registered title can be challenged and register can be corrected on the orders of the court. Therefore the conclusion is such as rotrust as in Australia.

Charges, Notices and Restrictions

To protect the rights of a third party over the registered land, there is a provision in the law to register charges, notices and restriction against a registered title. A registered title is subject to these charges, notices and restrictions entered in the register under various provisions of the Act.

Over-riding Interests

The registered title is not limited only by the registered interests but also by a whole lot of over-riding interests 'which do not appear in the register, yet bind the person who acquires any interest in registered land'.[27] As these interests are not registered, they cannot be discovered on inspection of the title register. Examples are rights of a person in possession of the property, lease of term less than seven years and fishing, shooting or hunting rights over a land. The interests defined in Schedule 1 over-ride the first registration and those defined in Schedule 3 over-ride the disposition of a registered estate. As mentioned earlier, the registration of a title is considered to have been introduced in England with the Land Registration Act, 1925. However, explanatory notes in LRA 2002 admit that LRA 1925 'does not clearly establish that a person can rely upon the register to say whether there are any limitations on the powers of a registered proprietor and safely act in reliance upon it.'[28] The reliance on the register is a basic feature of the title registration system which could not be ensured in England till 2002. The Land Registration Act, 2002 has reduced the over-riding interests in comparison to the 1925 Act but these are still not eliminated completely.

Alteration and Rectification in the Register

The provisions regarding alteration and rectification in the register on the grounds specified in Schedule 4 make a serious dent on the indefeasibility of a registered title. Making a provision for alteration and rectification is 'effectively a statement, that the register can be wrong. The Act also announces, as one of the grounds for alteration, 'correcting a mistake'. Such language is clearly at odds—at quite fundamental odds—with the idea that the register is conclusive.'[29] The provision allowing correction of a mistake has given rise to a lot of litigation leading to varied interpretations by courts regarding the circumstances allowing alteration and the effect of such alternation on the title of the registered proprietor.

Indemnity by the State

If a person suffers loss of his property due to any mistake in the register, he is provided compensation by the state. Indemnity is payable to the person who suffers loss due to rectification of the register or in case of a mistake whose correction would involve rectification of the register.[30] 'No indemnity is payable if the loss was suffered as a result wholly or partly of the claimant's own fraud. If however the loss was suffered as a result of the claimant's lack of proper care, then the indemnity payable is reduced to the extent that it is fair having regard to the claimant's share of the responsibility for the loss. Indemnity will not be payable when the claimant's lack of proper care is solely responsible for the loss.'[31] In England, an aggrieved person can directly file his claim before the Land Registry without any need to go to a civil court as is the case in Australia. If his claim is not accepted by the Land Registry, he has the right to appeal in the civil court.

Present Status of Registration in England and Wales

It is noteworthy that title registration laws were enacted almost at the same time in Australia and England. While registration was immensely successful in Australia, it had a rough journey in England. It took more than a century to achieve the first milestone of making registration compulsory in whole of England and Wales. The job is still far from complete. It is estimated that around 86 per cent of land in England and Wales is now registered, leaving about 14 per cent of land still unregistered.[32] In its journey of about one-and-a-half century towards establishment of a registration system, England has deployed the best of intellectual resources through a number of house committees, Royal Commissions and Law Commissions, that have produced many reports and legislations to achieve the goal of indefeasibility of a registered title. However, England is still far away from achieving 'title by registration alone' and 'indefeasibility of registered title' which was established in the states of Australia right in the beginning when Torrens laws were first enacted.

Experience of England with Title Registration

There are many scholarly studies on the reasons for the different levels of the success of title registration in Australian and England which give a wide spectrum of opinions on this subject. However, it is an undeniable fact that the there was a huge difference in the type of land tenures, law relating to property, structure of the courts and socio-economic conditions of the two countries at the time of introduction of the title registration law. The experience of England establishes very clearly that the success of title registration depends on many other ambient factors external to the Registration Act per se. The substantive law on property and the approach of the courts immensely influence the actual implementation of title registration in a country. Any country planning to switch over to title registration must be very careful in assessing these external factors and take suitable action to deal with them simultaneously to avoid failure

> **Box 6: Title Registration in England**
>
> 1. Before introduction of title registration in England, property transactions were done privately and not registered in any government record.
> 2. Title registration was introduced in 1862 but registration could effectively begin in 1925 after sweeping reforms were made in the law relating to property.
> 3. Registration could be made compulsory (that too at the time of the next transfer) in the whole of England and Wales in 1990 after about 125 years of its introduction. About 14 per cent land is still unregistered.
> 4. Unlike Australia, entry in the title register is not always indefeasible. It can be challenged and the register can be corrected on the orders of the court.
> 5. There are many 'overriding interests' that do not appear in the title register but affect the title of a buyer.
> 6. A person suffering loss due to incorrect registration is compensated by the government from the Indemnity Fund.

later. The difference in the title registration laws of England and Australia also indicates that there can be many variations of title registration law to suit the prevailing conditions in different countries.

Title Registration in Germany

The system of maintaining records of ownership and transactions in land in Germany is also classified as the title registration system though it is vastly different from the Australian and English systems. Due to these differences, while classifying the title registration systems existing in various countries, Dowson and Sheppard have kept Germany, Austria, Hungary, Poland, Czechoslovakia and Yugoslavia in a separate group and have named it as the 'German Group'. The other groups as per their classification are the English Group, the Torrens Group, the Swiss Group and the Ottoman Group.[33] In the context of India, a study of the German system assumes importance as it is based on an efficiently maintained cadastre which is similar to record-of-rights in India.

History of Title Registration

In Germany, registration of title was first adopted in Prussia with the enactment of the Prussian Land Register Code of 1872. This code formed the basis for extending land registration to the entire country in 1900. To introduce title registration in Germany, each of the state title registers were compiled on the basis of information available in the deed register and the cadastre and was published to invite claims and objections from the public. The title register was finalized after disposing of claims and objections received from the public.[34]

Law and Procedure for Title Registration

Unlike in Australia and England, the countries of continental Europe have a long tradition of maintaining cadastre, mainly for the purpose of collecting tax on land from the cultivators. Though cadastre originated for fiscal purposes, it had the potential to be used for keeping records of the title. Germany and a few other European countries have very effectively used the data available in the cadastre to maintain their title records. While many countries of continental Europe like France, Belgium and Italy continued with the deed registration system along with cadastre, Germany converted to the title registration system by using the deed register and cadastre in combination.

Numerus Clausus

German real property law follows the principle of *'numerus clausus'* which means that creation of rights in property cannot be left to the discretion of the parties involved in the transaction; they have to select from a pool of rights provided in the law. Following this principle, the law provides for an adequate pool of real rights which include 'servitudes, usufructs, land charges, right of pre-emption, priority cautions, hereditable building rights, property in a freehold flat, accessory mortgages and non-accessory land charges.'[35]

German Civil Code

The main legal body of German property law is codified in the German Civil Code (*Bürgerliches Gesetzbuch*-BGB). To supplement the principles contained in the Civil Code, procedural law is contained in the Land Registry Act (*Grandbuchordnung*-GBO) and The Regulation for Implementation of the Land Register (*Grundbuchverfügung*-GBV). The registration of transaction in the rights in the property involves two documents, viz., Land Register (*Grundbuch*) and Cadastre (*Liegenschaftskataster*).

Procedure for Registration

For the registration of ownership or any other right in the Land Register, the Land Registry Act prescribes four essential requirements. First, there should be an application either by the right holder or the beneficiary of the right. No change in the register can be initiated without an application for the same.[36] Secondly, the right holder should give his consent to make changes in the register.[37] Thirdly, the consent has to be verified by a notary to prove its authenticity. Fourthly, if ownership is being transferred, a deed executed before the notary has to be submitted along with an application for the registration.[38]

With these documents, an application for registration of ownership, mortgage or any other right can be presented before the registrar. The Registrar checks whether there is valid consent and whether the owner is already registered in the Land Register. No change in the register can be made unless the right proposed to be transferred is already registered in the name of the same owner who is giving consent for the transfer. If these requirements are fulfilled, the registrar makes changes in the register and informs the parties.

Generally transfer of property is split into two steps. After entering into a sale contract, a priority notice (*Vormerkung*) is registered with the registrar which ensures that nobody else can acquire that property till the priority notice is on record. After this, the buyer pays the sale price and possession is handed over to him by the seller. Now the notary submits the application for registration to complete the transfer of property.

Effect of Registration

Registration of land in the Land Register has a constitutive effect and a right in the land cannot be acquired without registration. All the transfers of ownership and other rights in land take effect only after being recorded in this Land Register as per prescribed procedure and therefore, this register at all the times shows the current status of title over a parcel of land. An entry in the Land Register gives rise to a presumption (*Vermutung*) that the rights registered belong to the person mentioned in the register and also that any right not mentioned in the register does not exist.[39] The Land Register enjoys 'public faith' which means that a transaction made on the basis of entries in the register will be considered a bonafide transaction even if entries were wrong. A person intending to purchase land can believe in the entries in the land register.

Indefeasibility of Registered Title

In Germany, there are no hidden rights which are not recorded in the land register. As the register is open to inspection by the public, it is the responsibility of a person whose interests are affected by a wrong entry to get it corrected. If he fails to do so and a person, without knowing the true position, buys the land from the registered owner, the title of the buyer is fully protected under the law. Under German law, the title of a bonafide buyer is 'untouchable and indestructible'.[40] However, if the buyer knew about the incorrect entry in the register, he loses absolute protection of his title and his title can be challenged through appropriate legal procedure.

However, if such a person further transfers this land to a bonafide buyer, the latter will be protected by the law.

Cadastre

In Germany, Cadastre is the 'official register of all the parcels and buildings in a state in which all parcels are described with graphical and textual data'.[41] Cadastre contains detailed information on each parcel of land like unique number, location, area, land use, details of the landowner, etc. A cadastral map, generally on the scale of 1:1000, showing all the parcels and their boundaries is also part of the cadastre. Each parcel is given a unique parcel number and the boundaries of each parcel are accurately defined based on a cadastral survey by authorised government agencies and licensed surveyors.

Land Register

In the Land Register, all the information, regarding ownership and other rights, is recorded with reference to a land parcel. A page (*Blatt*) of the German Land Register (*Grundbuch*) contains the following information for a particular land parcel:[42]

(i) Inventory (*Bestandsverzeichnis*), containing information about the property as mentioned in the cadastre, like parcel number, area, land use, etc.

(ii) Section I (*Abteilung I*), containing registration of owner and transfer of property.

(iii) Section II (*Abteilung II*), containing registration of encumbrances, easement and other such restrictions.

(iv) Section III (*Abteilung III*), containing mortgages, land charge, rent charge, etc.

In the Land Register, information on parcel number, location, area, land use, etc., is exactly the same as mentioned in the related Cadastre. Both the registers are constantly updated and kept in correspondence with each other. While the Land Register (*Grundbuch*) contains the legal status of all the parcels of land regarding ownership and other rights on the land, cadastre is an authentic record of parcel number, location, area and land use.

Institutional Structure

In Germany, different organizations are responsible for the maintenance of the Land Register and Cadastre. The former is part of the court system in Germany and is maintained by a registrar (*Rechtspfleger-RpflG*) under the supervision of the local district judge. The Land Register is governed by a federal law, viz. the Land Registry Act (GBO) which is applicable in all the states. The Cadastre is maintained by the surveying and cadastral authority of a state under its own legislation enacted for this purpose. Although the responsibility of maintenance of land register and cadastre is divided, the concerned agencies work in perfect coordination to ensure that both the registers are always kept in correspondence.

Principle of Abstract Nature of Rights

The German system of transfer of land is based on the principle of 'Abstraktionsprinzip' which distinguishes between an obligatory contract and consent to transfer the land. The contracts that place an obligation on the transferor to transfer the land or create some encumbrance on it are obligatory contracts. Agreements to sell a property or a loan agreement with a provision to create a mortgage in favour of the lender are examples of obligatory contracts. Though obligatory contracts are the basis for obtaining consent of the owner for transfer of ownership, the registrar acts solely on the strength of consent of the owner while registering the title. If a valid consent of the registered owner of property is presented before the registrar he does not go into the validity of the obligatory contract forming the basis of such consent.

The transfer and consequent registration is valid even if the obligatory contract is invalid. For example, registration of transfer of a property done with the consent of the owner will remain valid even if the agreed price is not paid by the buyer making the sale contract invalid. This principle is peculiar to German law but provides more certainty to the title of the land owner. While purchasing a property, the purchaser and his notary need not to look beyond the entry of the land register. The only option before a seller in such a contingency is to reclaim his property on grounds of unjust enrichment (*ungerechtfertigte Bereicherung*).[43]

Role of Notary

In Germany, the notary is regarded as a public officer and plays a very important role in the property transaction and registration. His services are invariably required for drafting most of the applications for registration. Also, the consent of the owner and the deed between the parties has to be executed before a notary as per requirement of law. Thus, there is double examination of transaction before any right is registered, first by the notary and secondly by the registrar. The notaries have to perform their duties as laid down in Federal Notary Law (*Bundesnotarordnung*) and Notarial Procedural Law (*Beurkundungsgesetz*).[44] It is the duty of the notary to give impartial advice to the parties regarding law and procedure and to explain the potential risks in the transaction. If a loss has been caused to a person due to negligence or wrong advice on the part of the notary, damages can be claimed against him. It is mandatory for all notaries to take malpractice insurance to take care of any such contingency.

Correction of Land Register

If the rights of any person are adversely affected due to an incorrect entry in the Land Register, he can apply for registration of an objection challenging its accuracy. Such objections can be registered on the basis of the consent of person whose right will be affected by the proposed correction or on the basis of an interim injunction of the court.[45] Registration of an objection acts as an alert to any person who wants to purchase the land under objection. If an application for registration of title on the land for which an objection has been registered is pending, the registrar advises the parties to settle the dispute before registration. Otherwise, the registration is done mentioning a contradiction as contained in the objection.[46] This contradiction may be removed on final disposal of the objection. Thus, a correction in the register can be made either with the consent of the registered owner or on the basis of facts proved in court.

In case it comes to the notice of the Land Registry that an entry has been made incorrectly which may lead to the true owner losing his right and consequent claim against the Registry, an ex-officio objection is entered in the register. This warns a bonafide purchaser of the incorrectness in the entry.[47] German law also provides for acquiring ownership by prescription to a person whose name appears in the register even if he is not a true owner of the property. A person who is wrongly registered as the owner of land and is also in possession of it acquires ownership if registration continues for thirty years without any objection from anyone.[48]

Indemnity for Loss

Unlike in the English and Torrens systems, there is no provision of indemnity to a person who suffers loss due to an incorrect entry in the Land Register. As has been described earlier, even if an entry in the Land Register is incorrect, a bonafide purchaser is protected and the land cannot be reverted to the true owner. Since there is no provision for an Assurance Fund as in Australia and England, a genuine land owner cannot make a claim for compensation to the registrar. However, as per the German Federal Constitution (*Grundgesetz*), the government is liable for the violation of duty by government officials. Therefore, if the loss has been caused due to mistake, negligence or a deliberate act on the part of officials of the land registry, an aggrieved person can claim damages from the government through the civil court.[49]

> **Box 7: Title Registration in Germany**
>
> 1. Germany converted to title registration in 1900 by using deed register and Cadastre in combination.
> 2. Title registration is part of the court system and is done under the supervision of the local district judge.
> 3. Like in India, Cadastre is maintained under state laws and registration is done under federal law.
> 4. There are no hidden rights (like over-riding interests in England) except those recorded in the land register.
> 5. Under German law, the title of a bonafide buyer is 'untouchable and indestructible.'
> 6. Unlike as in Australia and England, there is no fund to provide compensation to a person suffering loss due to incorrect registration. If loss is due to violation of duty by a government official, damages can be claimed against the government under general law.
> 7. If loss is due to negligence or wrong advice by a notary, damages can be claimed against him.

'Mirror', 'Curtain' and 'Insurance' Principles

Ruoff suggested that the success of a title registration system should be measured based on the extent to which it implements 'mirror', 'curtain' and 'insurance' principles. In the German system, land registration shows the updated status of legal rights because registration is constitutive and therefore compulsory. Any new acquisition of record is bound to get registered. Unlike as in England, there are no over-riding interests in Germany and therefore there are no rights outside the register affecting a registered title. Therefore, the German Land Register is closer to the true legal position than the Land Register in England. Sections 891 and 892 of the German Civil Code conform to the 'curtain' principle. Section 891 gives the presumption of truth to an entry in the land register which means that there is no need to look beyond the register. Further, Section 892 provides that 'contents of the land register shall be deemed to be correct' in favour of a person who acquires land bonafide. These provisions give a sound footing to the 'curtain' principle because with the protection provided by law a purchaser has no need to look behind the entries in the land register. However, the 'insurance' principle is non-existent in the German system. There is no insurance fund like Australia and England. An aggrieved person, though, can seek damages from the government through the civil court for the loss caused to him by the mistakes of the land registry.

NOTES

1. (Simpson 1976) p. 77
2. In New South Wales, Victoria and Tasmania, this system was introduced through their respective Real Property Acts in 1862, in Queensland through the Real Property Act, 1861, and in Western Australia through the Transfer of Land Act, 1875. The Northern Territory inherited the Torrens system from South Australia's Real Property Act, 1886 and later on enacted its own Real Property Act, 1978. In Australian Capital Territory, The Land Titles Act was enacted in 1925.
3. (European Discovery and the Colonisation of Australia 2017)
4. (Land Ownership-Old System) Land and Property Information
5. South Australia: Registration of Deeds Act, 1935(SA)
   Western Australia: Registration of Deeds Act, 1856(WA)
   States of Victoria, Queensland, Northern Territory and Capital Territory were created later and inherited laws of their parent states
6. (Simpson 1976) p. 72
7. (Real Property Act (SA) 1886), Sec. 51A
8. Ibid, Sec. 70
9. Ibid, Sec. 186
10. Ibid, Sec. 69 & 207
11. Ibid, Sec. 201
12. (O'Connor, Double Indemnity - Title Insurance and Torrens System 2003) p. 18
13. Lands granted before enactment of Torrens Laws which were allowed to remain under old deed registration system. These are also called General Law Lands.
14. (General Law Land)
15. (Simpson 1976) p. 197

16. (Land Titles) website of Victoria State government
17. 15 years in Victoria, 12 years in New South Wales and 20 years in Tasmania. (Sackville and Neave Australian Property Law p. 413)
18. (Land Registry Act, 1962) opening paragraph
19. (Simpson 1976) p. 43
20. (Land Transfer Act, 1875) opening paragraph
21. (Simpson 1976) p. 44
22. (Great Britain 1919) p. 10, para 23
23. (Sparkes 2016) p. 2
24. (Explanatory Notes, Land Registration Act, 2002) p. 2
25. Ibid, para 9, p. 2
26. (Land Registration Act, 2002) (Land Registration Act, 2002) sec. 58
27. (Explanatory Notes, Land Registration Act, 2002) p. 40 para 207
28. Ibid, p. 12 para 54
29. (Gardner 2014) p. 767
30. (Land Registration Act, 2002) sec. 103 and sch. 8
31. (Explanatory Notes , Land Registration Act, 2002) p. 53 para 282
32. (Updating the Land Registration Act, 2002: A Consultation Paper, Summary 2016) Law Commission England
33. (Simpson 1976) p. 77
34. (Simpson 1976) p. 123
35. (Wilsch 2012) p. 226
36. (Land Registry Act, Grandbuchordnung-GBO) Art. 13
37. Ibid, Art. 19
38. (Land Registry Act, Grandbuchordnung-GBO) Art. 20
39. (Real Property Law and Procedure in the European Union 2005) p. 15
40. (Wilsch 2012) p. 231
41. (Hawerk 1995) Para 4.1
42. (Real Property Law and Procedure in the European Union 2005) p. 13
43. Ibid, p. 20
44. Ibid, p. 11
45. (German Civil Code) (German Civil Code) secs. 894, 899
46. (Land Registry Act, Grandbuchordnung-GBO) sec.18
47. (Wilsch 2012) p. 230
48. (German Civil Code) (German Civil Code) sec. 900
49. (Wilsch 2012)

CHAPTER 5

Title Registration: Theory and Practice

Ruoff has laid down the 'mirror', 'curtain' and 'insurance' principles as defining features of a title registration system. The 'mirror' principle means that register accurately reflects all the material facts relating to title, the 'curtain' principle implies that for ascertaining the title no investigation beyond the register is necessary and the 'insurance' principle requires the state to guarantee the correctness of the register and to compensate any bonafide claimant suffering a loss due an incorrect entry in the register. However, these principles describe the ideal state which a title registration system of a country would try to achieve but in reality no country has ever achieved it. The degree to which each of these principles can be achieved depends on the actual provisions in the title registration law of each country. There is often a large a gap between the ideal state as laid down by these principles and the actual situation on the ground. In this section, various issues that prevent a country from implementing these principles fully have been discussed.

Mirror Works Other Way Round

The 'mirror' principle assumes that title recorded in the register is a true reflection of the legal rights. Actually, it is never so in reality. There are many interests that are recognised by law but not recorded in the title register. Further, due to genuine mistakes of the registrar or frauds played by fraudsters, a person other than the true owner may find a place in the title register. In the case of the death of an owner, the names of his heir/s may not appear in the register for a long time. A person holding an adverse possession has the right over the land but his right is not registered in the title register. So the register is not always a true image of the legal reality but by virtue of title registration law it is 'declared' to be the legal reality. Thus the 'mirror' principle works rather in an other way round where a supposed image is projected as the real object by the 'curtain' principle of the title registration.[1] Therefore, while assessing the usefulness of the title registration, it must be kept in mind that in no country's title register is the true image of the legal reality on a continuous basis. There are always certain differences between the legal reality and the title register which are dealt with as per provisions of the law in this regard.

Chinks in the 'Curtain'

The main feature of a title registration system is described as 'conclusiveness of registered title' which is mostly interpreted as indefeasible and unchallengeable and is a secured title. This characteristic of title registration immediately appeals to a country struggling with multiple problems in its land administration. On the face of it, title registration offers a panacea for all the problems regarding land disputes and related matters. It appears sometimes that once a conclusive and indefeasible title is written in the title register, all the litigation will just go away. However, the reality is something entirely different. Whatever adjective we ascribe to a registered title, it is as conclusive or as indefeasible as the actual legal provisions of the law make it. On going through title registration laws of various countries one finds that conclusiveness is not as robust as is made out by proponents of this system. The 'curtain' of the title registration system has many chinks in it.

Penny Carruthers has identified following exceptions to the indefeasibility in the Australian Torrens Acts:[2]

(i) Fraud exception where the current registered proprietor is guilty of fraud in obtaining registration.

(ii) 'Qualified indefeasibility' in relation to registered mortgages in Queensland, New South Wales and Victoria.

(iii) A registered proprietor's title can be challenged on the basis of an *in personam* claim.

(iv) The registrar's powers to correct the register.

(v) Overriding legislation.

(vi) Title of 'volunteer' registered proprietor is not indefeasible and is subject to the same unregistered claims that affected a donor's title.

John L. McCormack, a legal scholar who has studied land registration systems in depth, has observed that 'experience with title registration in the United States and elsewhere in common law countries indicates that conclusiveness of the register is an elusive, often unattainable goal.'[3] According to him, title register is never absolutely conclusive in any of the title registration systems. Some exceptions to the conclusiveness are always there in the law and some additional exceptions are sometimes created through court judgements. These fall into the following eight categories:[4]

(i) Caveats

(ii) Governmental interests

(iii) Private special interest exceptions

(iv) Possessory interests

(v) Equity

(vi) Error exception

(vii) Encroachment

(viii) Non-title related restrictions on ownership or use.

In many common law countries having title registration law, the civil courts have recognized unregistered rights as equitable interests which are against the concept of conclusiveness of the registered title.[5] Thus, though the title registration appears to provide complete security of title to the registered owner and to the buyer, 'in reality, there are gaps in the coverage provided by the State guarantee.'[6] Therefore, a change-over from the present system in India to the title registration system is not justified on the grounds that the title register will be absolutely conclusive and would offer complete security to a registered proprietor and a buyer of the property.

Limitations of State Indemnity

Title registration systems in many countries provide for a state-sponsored indemnity fund to compensate the genuine right holder who loses his right in the property due to the operation of the 'curtain' principle of the title registration law.

While in the deed registration system, a genuine but unregistered owner can recover his property from a registered owner, in the title registration system this is not possible due to the indefeasibility of the registered title. In such cases, the genuine owner can claim monetary compensation in lieu of his property. The experience of Australia and England shows that the procedure for claims from the indemnity fund is not as simple as it appears to be. As has been described in Chapter 4, in Australia a person gets a claim from the indemnity fund only when it is not possible to recover from the defaulter through court proceedings. This is called 'last resort' model which causes considerable hardship to the claimant. 'The provisions creating remedies against third parties are so complex that in some cases claimants have had difficulty identifying the right person to sue and the right remedy to pursue.'[7]

Many states in Australia have amended their laws to deny compensation in those cases where the loss is caused wholly or partly due to the negligence of the claimant. Thus, a genuine owner who loses his property due to the operation of title registration law is not assured of full compensation for his loss. In England, an indemnity claim can be directly submitted to the registrar but there are several limitations on such claims. No indemnity is payable if the loss was suffered as a result wholly or partly of the claimant's own fraud. If however the loss was suffered as a result of the claimant's lack of proper care, then the indemnity payable is reduced to the extent that it is fair having regard to the claimant's share of the responsibility for the loss. Indemnity will not be payable when the claimant's lack of proper care is solely responsible for the loss.[8]

Title Insurance in Countries with Title Registration

As described in Chapter 3, title insurance is the unique feature of the deed registration system of the USA where private insurance companies insure any defect in title of the seller. Ideally, title insurance should have no place in the title registration system because entries in the title register are conclusive proof of title and there should be no possibility of defect in the title due to 'mirror' and 'curtain' principles. Further, loss to a person due to a mistake in the register or subsequent rectification in the register is compensated by the state indemnity fund. However, in the USA

Box 8: Title Registration: Theory and Practice

1. 'Mirror', 'curtain' and 'insurance' principles describe an ideal state in a title registration system which no country has ever achieved.
2. Due to overriding interests, frauds, mistakes, non-recording of adverse possession, etc. the register is often not a true image of the legal reality.
3. In every title registration law there are exceptions to indefeasibility. So conclusiveness of the registered title is not as robust as it is made out to be.
4. Experience has shown that in case of loss, claim of compensation from the government is not simple. Claimants have to mostly first exhaust the option of the claim through a civil suit.
5. Title insurance business is expanding in Canada and Australia indicating lack of complete security in the title registration system.

title insurance is very common even in those jurisdictions where title registration is followed. The title insurance business is increasing in Canada and Australia also. This is an indication that title registration does not provide perfect security of title forcing people to go for additional security in the form of title insurance.[9]

NOTES

1. (J. A. Zevenbergen 2017)
2. (Carruthers 2015) p. 1265
3. (McCormack 1992) p. 61
4. (McCormack 1992) p. 90
5. (O'Connor, The Top 10 Legal Questions for Registered Title Systems 2010) p. 6
6. (O'Connor, Deferred and Immediate Indefeasibility: Bijural Ambiguity in Registered Land Title Systems 2009) p. 9
7. (O'Connor, Double Indemnity - Title Insurance and Torrens System 2003) p. 22
8. (Explanatory Notes, Land Registration Act, 2002) p. 52 para 282
9. (Zasloff 2011) p. 17

CHAPTER 6

Land Registration and Record-of-Rights in India

As per the most common terminology used in classification of registration systems, India falls in the category of deed registration countries. Registration of deed is conducted under the Registration Act, 1908 which is a law enacted by the central government. The substantial law on property is mainly contained in the Transfer of Property Act, 1882 which is also a central legislation. Unlike in many other deed registration countries, parcel-wise record-of-rights is also maintained in India, called record-of-rights, under the laws of the respective states. The record-of-rights in India is equivalent to cadastre,[1] which is the term used internationally for this kind of record.

Though India is classified as a deed registration country, it actually has two systems of maintaining a record of the ownership of property being operated by separate authorities under separate sets of laws. While documents relating to transfer of rights in the property are registered with the registrar under the Registration Act, 1908, land parcel-wise ownership records and cadastral maps are maintained by the revenue departments in each state. The present situation is aptly described by Kevin Nettle in the following words:[2]

> "India currently has two principal systems of land records with both a deed registration system and the land revenue system record-of-rights. Neither of these systems is complete or comprehensive or definitive. The record-of-rights is now basically only relevant to agricultural land. It has a spatial

framework but that framework may be weak and not up to date. The deeds registration system is intended to place on public record transactions with land in all areas but does not apply to certain matters affecting land ownership such as inheritance, transfers by operation of law, Court decrees, etc., although these matters can be recorded in the record-of-rights. This system is not map based and there are poor descriptions of property."

Therefore to understand the system of registration in India, registration law, state laws on record-of-rights and substantive law on property have to be studied together which has been done in this chapter.

Registration of Deeds

In India, registration of documents was first introduced in Bengal Presidency by the Bengal Regulation XXXVI of 1793. Subsequently, it was extended to Bombay Presidency by Regulation IV of 1802 and to Madras Presidency by Regulation XVII of 1802. Registration, however, was optional under these regulations. The Act of 1866 for the first time provided for compulsory registration of certain categories of documents. The Act of 1866 was replaced by Act III of 1872 which was subsequently replaced by the present Act XVI of 1908.[3]

All Property Transactions not Registered

The Registration Act makes registration of certain documents compulsory. In this category are included the instruments which affect right, title or interest in any immovable property. However, many documents that affect the rights in the immovable property like compromise decrees, grant of immovable property by the government, instrument of partition, instrument of collateral security for agricultural loans and a certificate of sale for property sold in public auction have been exempted from compulsory registration.[4] Further, certain documents executed by or in favour of government are deemed to be registered without being presented before the registrar and therefore these documents do not form part of the records of the registry.[5] Also, the registry does not have records of transfer of property through inheritance because such transfers are not required to be registered. Thus, all transactions relating to immovable properties do not reach the records of the registry and a prospective buyer has to look into other sources also to know the complete history of title of a property.

Effect of Registration

The registration of a deed has a constitutive effect as the Registration Act provides that no unregistered document that is required to be registered will have any effect on the immovable property comprised therein. Further, no such document will be received in the courts as evidence of affecting such property. This clearly means that a transaction in the property which has not been registered is invalid. This rule, however, is not applicable to property which is not required to be registered. Even in the case of documents for which registration is optional for the parties, a registered document will take effect against any unregistered document relating to the same property.[6]

Though a period of four months from the date of execution has been allowed for registration of a document, on registration, the document takes effect from the date of execution, irrespective of date of registration. Therefore, priority among the competing deeds relating to the same property is decided on the basis of date of execution and not on the date of registration. As per provisions of sec.48 of the Transfer of Property Act also, a deed executed earlier gets priority over a subsequently executed deed.

Procedure for Registration

All persons executing the document or their representatives, assigns or agents holding power of attorney, must appear before the registering officer. They have to admit execution and sign the document in the presence of the Registrar. Appearance may be simultaneous or at different times. If some of the persons are unable to appear within four months, further time up to an additional four months can be given on payment of a fine up to ten times the proper registration fee. On presentation of documents before him, the registrar makes an enquiry to satisfy himself that the document has actually been executed by the parties. The registrar can refuse registration only on very limited grounds one of them being denial of execution of document by any party. Grounds for refusal are given in sec 35(3). Incidentally, in France, the Netherlands and Germany, verification of the actual execution and identification of the parties is done by the notary only. The Registrar is not required to do this job there.

Indexes Maintained by the Registrar

The strength of any deed registration system depends on the ease with which a prospective buyer can search previous records of transactions relating to a particular property. A proper search can be made only if indexes are well organised and records are preserved efficiently allowing easy inspection. In India, all deeds affecting

---

Box 9: Deed Registration in India

1. Unlike as in France and the USA, deed registration has a constitutive effect in India. This is similar to the legal position in the Netherlands.
2. Many documents affecting rights in the immovable property have been exempted from compulsory registration in India.
3. The Registrar does not examine the legal validity of the transaction.
4. All the parties appear before the registrar who examines them to verify execution of the deed. In the Netherlands, France and Germany this verification is left to the notary.
5. In India, registration law provides for preparation of a grantor-grantee index as well as a tract index.

rights in immovable property are attached in Book No. 1. In respect of documents entered in Book No. 1, the Registrar is supposed to make two indexes. Index No. 1 contains the names of all the persons executing or claiming under a registered document, while Index No. 2 is a tract index listing all the documents arranged with respect to description of property. The tract index is very helpful in searching for the title history of a property. In the USA, a tract-wise index is provided in the registration acts of only a few states, mostly west of the Mississippi river and there also such indexes are not maintained. The absence of tract-wise index with the registrar in the USA has increased the dependence on the title insurance companies, who maintain tract-wise records for each property in a particular area.

Record-of-Rights

India has a long history of maintaining 'Record-of-Rights' for each village and city. This record has elaborate information on each parcel of land like ownership, possession, area, classification on the basis of soil quality and its use, land revenue (tax on land) and customary rights of the community. This record is maintained and updated by a well-established administrative machinery under the laws enacted by the respective state legislatures. The department of the state government that maintains these records is generally called the Revenue Department. Land revenue being a very insignificant part of total government income in present times, the only purpose of maintaining these records is to determine title and other rights of people over land.

The preparation of record-of-rights was begun in India by the British Government in the first half of the 19th century for the purpose of efficient assessment and collection of land revenue which constituted a major source of revenue for the Government. In 1841, the tax on land constituted 60 percent of the total revenue of the British government.[7] Correct assessment and collection of this tax required cadastral survey of the whole area, classification of soil conditions, identification of the owner responsible for payment of revenue and fixation of boundaries of each field. Therefore, the British established a strong administrative machinery from the government headquarters to the village level whose job was to meticulously survey and classify each piece of land and assess the correct land revenue to be paid by the proprietor or tenant on the land. Specific laws were enacted and detailed procedural manuals were developed to guide the officials engaged in this work.

Utility of Record-of-Rights

'After independence, the share of land revenue in state resource inflows declined drastically, from more than 30% in the late 1950s to less than 2% in the late 1980s'.[8] In spite of a negligible share of the land revenue in their income, state governments spend a huge amount of money and effort to maintain and update record-of-rights because of its utility to the public and the government. After independence, almost all the states implemented land reforms with the objective of giving ownership of agricultural land to the actual tiller and distributing surplus land to the landless. Just to mention some achievements in this regard, about 12.5 million tenants have got their rights protected over 16.5 million acres of land, 4.9 million acres of land has been seized from big landowners and distributed to 5.4 million landless farmers and another 14.8 million acres of government wasteland has been granted to the landless rural poor.[9] All these reform measures have been implemented on the basis of the record-of-rights which is the only record giving information on ownership and tenancy on each parcel of the land.

A Comprehensive Parcel-wise Record on Land Title

Sometimes, while assessing the system of registration in India, attention is paid only to the registration of deeds and the records maintained by the registrars under the Registration Act, 1908. The indexes and records maintained by the registrars have many limitations which any deed registration system would have because of the very nature of working of a registry and the inherent

> **Box 10: Analysis of Laws on Record of Rights in Select States**
>
> In Appendix-A, enactments relating to record-of-rights of Maharashtra, Karnataka, Punjab and West Bengal have been analysed on the following common parameters:
>
> 1. Coverage of urban area
> 2. Contents of record-of-rights
> 3. Legal sanctity
> 4. Administrative machinery
> 5. Preparation of records, cadastral survey and involvement of the community
> 6. Public access to records
> 7. Regular updating of records
> 8. Adjudication procedures
> 9. Role of civil courts

limitations of a law for registration of deed. Therefore, in India, records of the registry do not give a complete picture of the title over land.

The record-of-rights, though maintained by state authorities, is an integral part of the title records eco-system in India. Record-of-rights is the only document which records title and possession with respect to each parcel of land and is updated for all types of transactions in property like sale, purchase, succession, grants by the government, decree of the courts, etc. Many of these transactions are not required to be registered and therefore never become part of the records of the deed registry. On the contrary, every change in the ownership of a property has to be compulsorily informed to the concerned authorities for making requisite changes in the record-of-rights. Therefore, if maintained strictly as per provisions of the law, record-of-rights gives a more comprehensive status of title on a property.

In India, while deed registration is done under a central law (Registration Act, 1908), all the states have their own laws to maintain records-of-right. This position is similar to that prevailing in Germany where the Land Register is made under a federal law and the cadastre (equivalent of the Indian record-of-rights) is maintained under state-specific laws.

Detailed Analysis of Record-of-Rights in Four States

In this book, enactments of four states, viz., Punjab, Maharashtra, Karnataka and West Bengal have been taken up for detailed analysis. These states represent all the four regions of the country, i.e., North, South, East and West. They also represent three main systems of land revenue collection introduced by the British in India. Punjab was under *Mahalwari* system, West Bengal was under *Zamindari* system and *Raiyatwari* system prevailed in most parts of Maharashtra and Karnataka. A detailed analysis of the laws of these four states has been done on certain common parameters which, having a direct bearing on the preparation and maintenance of record-of-rights, are relevant for this study. This analysis is given at **Appendix-A**. The provisions in the laws of other states are largely on the same pattern with minor differences. Based on this analysis, certain common characteristics of record-of-rights have been described in the following paragraphs.

Contents of Record-of-Rights

Almost all the land over which private rights exist has been surveyed in India with unique identification numbers allotted to each land parcel. There are two ways in which spatial information on land has been organized in India.[10] In the northern, eastern, western and north-eastern states, cadastral maps on a fairly large scale ranging from 1:500 to 1:5000 are prepared, while in the southern states, maps of individual parcels, called '*Tippan*' are made from the spatial measurements recorded in the Field Measurement Book.[11] In the states where *Tippan* and Field Measurement Book are maintained as basic spatial records, an index map on a smaller scale is also prepared for reference purposes. The laws of the states provide for making a record-of-rights in cities as well as in villages. The textual record has reference of the unique number allotted to each parcel of land to identify the property. The textual records generally consist of a record of ownership, possession, tenancy and present use for each parcel of land. A document mentioning easement rights, community rights and other common interests is also maintained as part of record-of-rights.

Process of Preparing Record-of-Rights

These records are prepared through a legal process of survey and settlement which is taken up periodically as per the requirement of a particular area. During this process, the officials of state governments visit each and every land parcel, plot it on the map and record the ownership, possession and other details required to be included in the record-of-rights. These details are recorded on the basis of local enquiry, transfer deeds, documents of government grants, court orders and any previous record-of-rights. The draft record so prepared is published for general information and copies are supplied to the right holders for making representations which are disposed of by designated officers as per laid down procedures. Finally, the record is read out in an assembly of right holders of that area before final attestation.

Updating of Record-of-Rights

To ensure regular updating of records, any person acquiring a right through a conveyance deed, inheritance, court decree or by any other means is duty bound to report such acquisition to the designated official within a prescribed time, with a penalty for any delay in this regard. In Maharashtra and Karnataka, the duty to send information on the registered conveyance deeds and government grants has been assigned to the registrar and district collector, respectively, instead of the right holder. In Karnataka, a civil court is also required to send a copy of the decree affecting the rights in land to the officer responsible for the maintenance of the record-of-rights. On the basis of information given by the right holder or other agencies, a mutation is entered in a register which is basically a proposal to make changes in the record-of-rights. This proposal is inquired into as per laid down procedures which necessarily include hearing all the affected parties. If after the inquiry, changes are approved by the designated officer, they are incorporated in the record-of-rights; otherwise the claimant is informed about rejection of his claim.

Adjudication Process

A person not satisfied with the order of a designated officer has the option to appeal against this order to the higher authorities as per provisions of the law. The officers holding an inquiry into disputes regarding an entry to be made in the record-of-rights are adequately empowered with powers of the civil courts for enforcing the attendance of witnesses and taking evidence. The parties can be represented by an advocate and have the opportunity to appeal against an order adversely affecting their interests. Civil courts are barred from interfering in the process of making or updating record-of-rights. However, a civil court can adjudicate on the rights of an individual in relation to land in a suit for declaration, which is somewhat similar to 'quiet title action' in the USA. The record-of-rights is updated as per the decision of the court in such a suit for declaration.

Presumption of Correctness

In all the state laws relating to record-of-rights, there is a specific provision that an entry in the records will be presumed to be true unless proved otherwise, which means that rights mentioned in the record-of-rights are correct unless someone produces enough evidence to prove them wrong. This provision is similar to the provision in German Civil Code (*Bürgerliches Gesetzbuch*, BGB) which reads: 'the contents of the land register shall be deemed to be correct, unless a contradiction is recorded against the correctness or the inaccuracy is known to the acquirer.'

On going through the analysis of state laws at **Appendix-A**, which has been summarized in the previous paragraphs, it can easily be inferred that the record-of-rights in India contains comprehensive information on ownership and other rights of persons on the land. Further, information on rights is linked to a cadastral map which shows each and every land parcel. Thus record-of-rights in India is a cadastre combined with record of title which is comparable to the Land Register (*Grandbuch*) in Germany. Like in Germany, almost all the land over which private rights exist has been surveyed with unique identification numbers allotted to each land parcel. The record-of-rights has been made with reference to these parcel identification numbers which makes it very easy to ascertain the status of rights on any land parcel. This kind of comprehensive cadastre containing all the land parcels of the country does not exist in England or Australia who are following the title registration system. The USA which follows deed registration system also does not have this kind of cadastre.

To summarize, the most important features of record-of-rights in India are that it is mandatory for everyone to get his newly acquired right recorded; records are changed only after detailed inquiry; rights over all the land in the country are compiled with reference to unique parcel numbers and presumption of truth is attached to the entries in these records. These attributes make record-of-rights a reliable public document which can be further improved to provide a strong land administration system. The World Bank report 'India Land Policies for Growth and Poverty Reduction' mentions the following about record-of-rights in India:

> 'Contrary to many developing countries where cadastral databases do not exist and have to be created from scratch, one of the great advantages of India is that the spatial record

created by the British, in the form of village maps and FMBs, is surprisingly accurate and main problems of the spatial database are due to lack of updating or wholesale change of land use.'[12]

The record-of-rights is often criticised by some writers as being outdated, inaccurate and of no utility. However, most of these comments are not based on the systematic study of record-of-rights but on a few individual experiences in some particular area of the country. With India being a vast country having more than 250 million land parcels,[13] it is possible that records in many places may not be maintained to the required standards, but on the basis of a few examples a sound system of land administration cannot be written off completely.

Box 11: Record-of-Rights in India

1. Record-of-rights in India is equivalent to Cadastre in European countries.
2. The law provides for maintenance of record-of-rights both in urban and rural areas.
3. Under the law, every change in ownership has to be compulsorily informed to the revenue officer for updating the record-of-rights.
4. In disputed cases, changes in the record-of-rights are made only after adjudication by a quasi-judicial authority.
5. Entries in the record-of-rights are presumed to be correct unless proved otherwise.
6. Record-of-rights has ownership recorded against uniquely identifiable land parcels. Such parcel-wise record was not available in Australia and England before introduction of title registration.

Law on Transfer of Property

The substantive law on transfer of property in India is contained in the Transfer of Property Act, 1882. This enactment lays down general principles as well as detailed rules regarding transfer of property by sale, mortgage, lease, exchange and gift between living beings. After the enactment in 1882, this legislation was amended 12 times till 1929 when it was revised most comprehensively. However after that, in the next more than 80 years, only a minor amendment has been done in 2002. In any endeavour to reform the land markets to bring them in tune with economic realities of modern India, the policy makers must relook at this 135-year-old legislation. Whether India adopts title registration, as is being recommended by the central government, or continues with the present deed registration system, substantive law on property would always play a major role in imparting certainty to the title and reducing unnecessary litigation. In this chapter some important provisions of this law, having a bearing on land registration have been discussed.

History of Law on Transfer of Property

To appreciate the Transfer of Property Act rightly, a quick look into the history of this enactment would be of immense help. Before the advent of the British, the various communities in India were following their own customary laws in various civil matters including transfer of property. In the middle of the 19th century the British rulers were grappling with the problem of establishing a formal legal system in British India. 'It was not clear how far the English law applied, even in the Presidency Towns. In the celebrated case of Mayor of Lyons v. East India Company, Lord Brougham expressed the opinion that the Indian inhabitants were governed by their own laws and that the English law applied only to British subjects and other foreigners'.[14] In areas other than the Presidency towns, various regulations directed the courts to decide the cases according to 'justice, equity and good conscience.'

England did not have a codified law on civil matters at that time and their jurisprudence was based on 'common law', i.e., principles laid down by the courts through their judgments which worked as a precedent for decisions in future cases. Accepting the view of Lord Macaulay that 'no country ever stood so much in need of a code of law as India,' the British Parliament decided to draft a comprehensive Indian Code covering all the possible aspects of civil law. The draft of the Transfer of Property Act prepared by the Third Law Commission, was intended to be one of the chapters of the Indian Code with considerable rearrangement of the sections. However, the ambitious project of enacting a self-contained Indian Code never materialized and the Transfer of Property Act was enacted by making it self-contained as far as possible.[15] This is perhaps the reason that this law has no comprehensive definition of property and has a peculiar provision that 'The chapters and sections of this Act which relate to contracts shall be taken as part of the Indian Contract Act, 1872 (9 of 1872). And section 54, paragraphs 2 and 3, sections 59, 107 and 123 shall be read as supplemental to the Indian Registration Act, 1908 (16 of 1908).'[16]

Influence of English Law

Though the stated objective of the codification of property law for India was to adapt English common law to local customary law, the Transfer of Property Act drew heavily upon English law at that time. Not only the common law but the principles of equity also have so much influence on this enactment that 'hardly any important section of the Act can be understood in its true sense without a background of the relevant principles of equity.'[17] It is common knowledge that in the 19th century, the absence of a codified law and simultaneous existence of common law and principles of equity had made land law in England very complex and beyond the comprehension of ordinary citizens. Joshua Williams, writer of the leading textbook in England, 'Williams on Real Property,' said about English land law in 1878 that 'some of the most remarkable of these laws, viewed by themselves, apart from their history, and judged only by the benefits which now result from them, appear to me to be absolutely worthless. Others are more than worthless, they are absurd and injurious'.[18]

The complexities of English land law have obviously crept into Indian property law also which, therefore, requires a relook to bring it in line with present times. Before taking up specific provisions of this Act for discussion, an observation of Justice V.R. Krishna Iyer cannot but be quoted here. He has observed that the 'Transfer of Property Act, although ancient in origin, has undergone thorough mutation in 1929, more to bring it in accord with the principles of English Law. However, it must be remembered that English Law is not applicable to India now and we have to go by Indian conditions and the text of Indian statutes.'[19]

Applicability of Transfer of Property Act

As per sec. 2, nothing in chapter II of the Act 'shall be deemed to affect any rule of Mohammedan law.' The transfer of immovable property creates *'jus in rem,'* i.e., right enforceable against anyone in the world and therefore it should be based on the principles explicitly laid down in the law which can be understood by everyone. Chapter II of the Act contains important principles regarding transfer of property like what can be transferred, person competent to transfer, rule against perpetuity, conditional transfer, transfer by co-owner, etc., and making these provisions subject to Mohammedan law, which is largely un-codified, is bound to create uncertainty about the validity of a transaction especially when parties to the transfer may be from different religions.

Conditional Transfer of Property

This act allows an owner of a property to dispose it of either absolutely or conditionally incorporating a salutary principle that the law favours freedom of transfer of property.[20] However, at the time of transfer of property, an owner is allowed to impose conditions on use, transfer and obligations of transferee. Secs. 11 to

34 of the Act lay down the principles regarding valid and invalid conditions, their effect on the rights of the transferee and related issues. A few of the valid conditions in these sections are: the interest transferred taking effect only on happening of a specified uncertain event (sec. 23); while transferring property to one person, an ulterior disposition of same property by same transaction to another person if disposition to first person fails (sec. 27); transferring property to one person with condition that property will pass on to another person in case of a specified uncertain event (sec. 28); condition that transfer shall cease to have effect in case of happening of specified uncertain event (sec. 31). A somewhat similar provision is there in the case of a gift also where, on the happening of any specified event, the gift can be suspended or revoked (sec. 126). 'The influence of English legal concepts is clearly seen in the structure and terminology of these sections.'[21] It is worthwhile to mention that owing to the inherent flexibility of common law, English legal concepts have evolved over the years through court rulings with the changing needs of society. However, in India, these concepts were made part of statutory law way back in the 19th century and therefore cannot evolve except by an amendment in the law by Parliament.

The legal sanction of conditional transfer, gives absolute freedom to the current owner in the matter of disposition of his property but it destroys the freedom of subsequent owner in the disposition of the same property. The concept of imposition of conditions on transfer which includes sale, lease, mortgage and gift (sec. 5) goes against the free alienability of immobile property which is essential for a modern land market. Therefore, the concept of conditional transfer of immovable property requires a thorough review in the context of present-day socio-economic requirements.

The rules for valid and invalid conditions, whether a condition is required to be fulfilled 'substantially' or 'strictly', whether the happening of a specified uncertain event has become impossible and other such concepts contained in this legislation are not amenable to easy interpretation leading to a huge mass of case laws on this subject. The result of the application of these principles will change substantially with a slight variation in the facts of the case. An illustration given in sec. 27 of the Act is quoted below to clarify this point:

> 'A transfers property to his wife; but, in case she should die in his life-time, transfers to B that which he had transferred to her. A and his wife perish together, under circumstances, which make it impossible to prove, that she died before him. The disposition in favour of B does not take effect.'

As per the circumstances stated in the illustration, B does not get the property. However, if B is able to prove, with the help of advanced medical technology, that the wife had died even a fraction of second before A, he will get the property. These circumstances are likely to lead to prolonged litigation between B and the natural heirs of A. As such, the issues can be adjudicated by a civil court only and the title to this property will remain uncertain till the case is decided and the property will not be alienable further.

This kind of provisions making the title of a person to immovable property dependent on certain conditions subsequent to the transfer render the title uncertain to the extent of being indeterminable in certain cases and therefore are not in consonance with the present thinking of making land as a freely marketable commodity. These provisions are actually vestiges of old English land law which evolved over the centuries from feudal origins. 'In England, a land owning aristocracy had an intense desire to rule posterity from the grave. They strove to keep their large estates tied up in their families forever, and their families, with equal vigour, strove to free themselves.'[22] In England, a transaction in immovable property was a private affair closely guarded from public eye by the land aristocracy which opposed any kind of registration of the transaction in a public record. However, in India, almost every transfer in immovable property is to be registered under the Registration Act which has the effect of giving notice to the world about the new acquisition of right in the property. These principles of conditional transfer have the effect of altering the title subsequently without any notice to the world.

Transfer by Person Other than Owner

There is another class of provisions in the Act which has the potential to create uncertainty to the title of immovable property, i.e., transfer of property by a person other than the true owner or his agent. These rules contained in secs. 35, 38, 41 and 43 provide that in certain conditions such transfer can be legitimised. Without going into the detail of each of these rules, it is sufficient to say that in the interest of certainty to title and free marketability of land, no such contingency should be allowed by law and it should be clearly laid down that all transfers done by an unauthorised person will be void. Any such transfers may create any obligation between the parties regarding monetary compensation but it should in no way affect the right in property.

Mortgages

The Transfer of Property Act, 1882 has Chapter IV exclusively devoted to mortgages of immovable property which describes six types of mortgages and rights and obligations of mortgager, mortgagee and any third party transacting in the land under mortgage. The relevance of these provisions in the present economic scenario where most of the credit flows from formal institutions like banks and non-banking financial companies (NBFC) requires a review. These institutions provide credit on the basis of formal mortgage instruments with terms and conditions in conformity with the policies laid down by the Reserve Bank of India or the Government of India. In such type of mortgages, the provisions laid down in the Act in so much detail would, perhaps, never be required.

Mortgage by Deposit of Deeds

The Act provides for creation of mortgage by deposit of deeds without executing any deed or any kind of registration. This provision is being used extensively by financial institutions because of simplicity of procedure and savings on registration fee and stamp duty. However, this provision gives rise to the possibility of fraud by selling the mortgaged property on the basis of forged documents. The prospective buyer would not know about such mortgage as there is no record in the registry. Therefore, mortgage by deposit of title deeds should either not be allowed or at least a memorandum regarding deposit of deeds should be registered with the registrar at a nominal fee.

Strengths of Indian System

A typical title registration system has the following features:

(i) A register which contains rights of people written against a particular land parcel.

(ii) A map of all the land parcels appearing in the register with their unique identity.

(iii) Legal provision that the right will be transferred only on registration in the register. This is also referred to as 'constitutive' character of registration.

(iv) Legal provision that entry in the register will be assumed to be correct and a person buying land on the basis of that entry will get legal protection even if the entry is found incorrect later on.

(v) A provision for compensating a person who suffers loss due to incorrect entries in the records.

The Indian system with the combination of deed registration and record-of-rights already has some of these features. This issue is further elaborated in the following paragraphs.

Land Parcel-wise Record-of-Rights

In addition to records of the deed registry, a comprehensive land parcel-wise record of ownership exists in the form of record-of-rights. The law provides for recording of all land-related transactions in this record. This record is updated following a quasi-judicial process. This kind of land parcel-wise record is not available in many other countries having deed registration system.

Constitutive Effect of Deed Registration

This is an important feature of title registration system. In title registration countries like Australia, England and Germany, a right in land takes legal effect only after entry is made in the title register. Due to this feature, a title registration system is often described as 'title by registration' in contrast to 'registration of title' in a typical deed registration system. In a typical deed registration system, including that of France and the USA, right is transferred as soon as deed is executed by the parties. Registration of deed is required only for its enforceability against third parties. However, Indian deed registration law goes a step further and makes deed registration constitutive. The Registration Act, 1908 provides in unambiguous terms that no document required to be registered under the Registration Act or the Transfer of Property Act shall affect any immovable property comprised therein unless it has been registered.[23] Thus, a transaction has no legal effect on the property without registration of a deed for such transaction (except for transactions which are not required to be registered under the law). This feature of Indian law is similar to that in the Netherlands where also title is not transferred until the deed is registered in the registry.

Further, it is also compulsory for a person acquiring right in a property to get his right recorded in the record-of-rights (cadastre). The only shortcoming in the Indian system is that transactions of property through registration of deeds are not expeditiously recorded in the record-of-rights, though such recording is mandatory under the law. This shortcoming is entirely attributable to the lack of implementation of law.

Presumption of Truth to Record-of-Rights

Recording of rights with reference to a land parcel supported by a map of the parcel is the most fundamental feature of a title registration system. In India, in addition to deed registration there is the tradition of making record-of-rights (Cadastre) where all the rights are recorded against a particular parcel of land. Also, there is system of making cadastral maps having the unique identity of each parcel. Laws of the states regarding making of cadastre make it mandatory for everyone to get his newly-acquired right in the cadastre. It is true that initially record-of-rights was made for the fiscal purpose of collecting land revenue but presently it is being used for the recording of rights of the people on the land. It is maintained under laws made by state legislatures and entries in the record-of-rights actually give legal status of the rights of people over land. The entries in the cadastre have been granted 'presumption of truth' under the law which means that these entries can be negated only on the basis of reliable evidence. Thus, in India, the first two features of a title registration system already exist, which was not the case in Australia and England when title registration was first introduced there.

Search of Records of Registry

One of the advantages of a title registration system over a deed registration system is the better management of property-wise records and easy retrieval of information whenever required. While comparing the two systems, difficulty in searching old title records of a particular property in deed registries is most often cited as justification for adoption of the title registration system. This is true to some extent because it is a well-known fact that searching through title records of a particular property in the deed registry involves considerable time, effort and expenditure on the part of the prospective buyer.

However, in India, the situation is better than a typical deed registration system as exists in the USA. In India, the Registration Act provides for making tract-wise indexes as well as grantor-grantee indexes. This makes the search of records of a particular property somewhat easier. Further, as per law, all the transactions in a property have to be recorded in the cadastre (record-of-rights) against a particular property. The record-of-rights effectively works as a tract-wise index and greatly helps a prospective buyer to search previous ownership records of a property.

Encumbrance Certificate

In most of the states, the law provides for the issue of an encumbrance certificate by the registrar on demand for a particular property. The encumbrance certificate is an official search report regarding the title of a particular property on the basis of records maintained in the registry. It is the duty of the registrar to mention all the registered transactions in respect of a particular property in the encumbrance certificate. Many states have computerized their registries and have started issuing this certificate online. Thus, a search of the title of a property in India is simpler than in a typical deed registration system like that of the USA.

Protection to a bonafide Buyer

In the title registration system, the law protects a bonafide buyer of the property on the basis of entries in the title register even if those entries are found incorrect later. This feature is the most important difference between deed registration and title registration systems. As a principle, this protection is not available in the deed registration system where the title of even a bonafide buyer is not protected, if the title of the seller is found defective at any time after the sale. This feature, called dynamic security of title, has far-reaching consequences on the rights of the people. How far this principle can be implemented will depend not only on the existing law and jurisprudence but also on the fundamental concepts of fairness in a country. It is a conscious choice to be made by a country as to how far a bonafide buyer can be protected at the cost of the true owner of the property.

Under Indian law, a bonafide purchaser acting in good faith has not been left totally unprotected. The provisions contained in Part B of Chapter II of the Transfer of Property Act, 1882 provide some protection against undetected defects in the title of the seller and undetected encumbrances on the land.

Problems in the Present System

To identify the problems with the present system of registration of property in India, the available literature where experts have recommended a change-over to title registration has been reviewed. D.C. Wadhwa in his articles 'Guaranteeing Title to Land—A Preliminary Study'[24] and 'Guaranteeing Title to Land—The Only Sensible Solution'[25] has observed that under the deed registration system as practised in India, a sale deed is only an evidence of transaction and not conclusive proof of title. Also, an entry in the record-of-rights is not conclusive proof of a title because the government does not guarantee the title as recorded in the record-of-rights. The ownership of a person recorded in the record-of-rights is only presumptive and can be challenged on various grounds.

He has identified the following problems relating to land administration in India:

(a) In all parts of the country, land records are in a very bad shape. These are not updated timely; hence, they do not show the correct status of ownership. There is no authentic map of any urban agglomeration in the country. The poor farmer has nothing to prove his ownership except by entry in the land records and his title is vulnerable.

(b) In many cases, the government, public bodies and private persons owning the land as per record-of-rights are not in possession of those lands. Many persons in possession of the land do not find mention in the record-of-rights.

(c) This situation has led to incessant litigation and clogging of judicial machinery.

Swati Ramanathan in her article 'Security of Title to Land in Urban Areas' published in India Infrastructure Report 2009 has recommended the adoption of of a state-guaranteed title registration system in India, especially in urban areas because lack of clarity on records and rights impacts urban policies, urban planning and urban management. She observes that 'what we have in India today is a presumed ownership to land which is questionable and can be challenged on multiple fronts: ownership, extent of boundaries, financial encumbrances, inheritance subdivisions, etc.'[26] The main problems in the present system as identified by her can be summarized thus:

(i) The Revenue Department has no role in urban areas. Mutations are not done and records are not updated. Lawyers have to look through registration records and tax records to know the position of title.

(ii) No compulsory registration of land-related transactions which weakens the authenticity of records.

(iii) Non-availability of land free of litigation for developing housing and infrastructure in urban areas. In urban areas, records are not updated to account for new transactions and therefore there are no comprehensive record-of-rights on the basis of which ownership can be verified with certainty.

(iv) Increasing social cost of enormous delays in land-related disputes.

(v) Inadequate management of land records also results in corruption, patronage and inefficient delivery systems.

In the guidelines of the National Land Records Modernization Programme, the reasons for taking a decision to change-over to title registration are not given. However, a paper by Smt. Rita Sinha, the then Secretary, Department of Land Resources, Government of India, gives an insight into the background of this policy decision.[27] She has mentioned the following problems with the present system:

(i) Outdated cadastral maps and arrears of data entry in the record-of-rights. The records do not reliably reflect reality.

(ii) At the time of registration of a deed regarding a land transaction, past ownership has to be probed to establish non-encumbrance.

(iii) Litigation is the bane of presumptive titling in India. Litigation will be considerably reduced once titles are conclusive.

Thus, the main problems identified by experts are poorly updated land records especially in urban area, heavy litigation, difficulty in assessing the encumbrance on land at the time of purchase and an inefficient delivery system. Title registration has been recommended with the assumption that all these problems are due to the inherent shortcomings of the deed registration system and can only be solved by a change-over to the title registration system. However, most of the problems identified by experts relate to poor implementation of existing laws and procedures which can be improved without going for an altogether new system.

As has been mentioned earlier, both the systems are working successfully around the world and a country has to select a system suitable for its own social, economic and legal environment. An important decision like changing a well-established land registration system should not be taken without a detailed objective analysis of the current problems and without being reasonably certain that the new system will solve those problems. India actually has two sub-systems, viz., deed registration and record-of-rights, for the purpose of recording the rights of people over property. This places the Indian deed registration system on a better footing in comparison to the deed registration systems in many other countries. Before deciding on the issue of requirement and suitability of a title registration system for India, it would be prudent to understand the real difference between the two systems. The Indian system has many features that are closer to the features of a title registration system and therefore the adoption of a title registration may not add much value to the existing system.

NOTES

1. A Cadastre is normally a parcel based, and an up-to-date land information system containing a record of interests in land (e.g. rights, restrictions and responsibilities). It usually includes a geometric description of land parcels linked to other records describing the nature of the interests, the ownership or control of those interests, and often the value of the parcel and its improvements. (Definition of cadastre by the International Federation of Surveyors)
2. (Nettle 2006)
3. (Law Commission of India 1957) p. 1
4. (The Registration Act, 1908), Sec. 17
5. (The Registration Act, 1908), Sec 90
6. (The Registration Act, 1908) Secs. 49, 50
7. (Iyer 2005) p. 1192
8. (World Bank 2007) p. 8
9. (Annual Report, Ministry of Rural Development 2006-07)
10. (The National Land Records Modernization Programme, Guidelines, Technical Manuals and MIS 2008-09)
11. (Sinha 2010) p. 18
12. (World Bank 2007) p. 24
13. (World Bank 2007) p. 3
14. (Law Commission of India 1977) p. 11
15. (Law Commission of India 1977) p. 11
16. (The Transfer of Property Act, 1882) Sec. 4
17. (Law Commission of India 1977), p. 15
18. (Simpson 1976) p. 25
19. (Krishna Iyer 2001)
20. (The Transfer of Property Act, 1882), Sec. 7
21. (Law Commission of India 1977)
22. (Simpson 1976) p. 25
23. (The Registration Act, 1908) sec. 49
24. (Wadhwa, *Guaranteeing Title to Land: A Preliminary Study* 1989)
25. (Wadhwa, *EPW* 2002)
26. (Ramanathan 2009), p. 22
27. (Sinha 2010)

CHAPTER 7

Relevance of Title Registration in India

Introduction of conclusive title in respect of property in India has been under discussion since long. Some experts believe that the only solution to the problems related to land markets and land administration in India is the introduction of a system of 'conclusive title' on property in place of the existing system. As the chairman of One-man Committee on Record-of-Rights in Land, D.C. Wadhwa in his report submitted to the Planning Commission in 1989 recommended replacing the present system of presumptive rights over land with the system of conclusive title. The Venkatachaliah Commission also recommended 'state guarantee of private and public land' as one of the administrative reforms.[1]

The Department of Land Resources, Government of India, has launched the National Land Records Modernization Program (NLRMP) in 2008 to 'modernize management of land records, minimize scope of land/property disputes, enhance transparency in the land records maintenance system and facilitate moving eventually towards guaranteed conclusive titles to immovable properties in the country.'[2]

Under the scheme of division of subjects between the Union Government and the state governments under the Constitution of India, 'maintenance of land records' and 'survey for revenue purposes and records of rights' are state subjects. Therefore any law relating to registration of conclusive title has to be enacted by the states only. While considerable progress has been made by the states in the implementation of other components of NLRMP, they have not done much towards introduction of conclusive titling in the states.

Thus, as the situation exists today, the Department of Land Resources, Government of India, has taken a policy decision to change-over to the system of conclusive title in the country. As per the constitutional division of powers and responsibilities, action for implementation of this policy can be initiated by the states only and they are not very confident in going in for such a massive change in the legal system. Because of this, the issue frequently finds mention in the reports of experts and policies of the government, but not much is happening on the ground.

For the purpose of introducing title registration in the country, the Department of Land Resources, Government of India, has circulated a Draft Land Title bill 2011[3] seeking public opinion. This Bill envisages wide-ranging changes in the existing institutional structure for management of registration and title records. Apart from changes in the institutional structure, change-over to the title registration system will also require the introduction of new legal principles in the jurisprudence of the country.

The experience of other countries has demonstrated that implementation of title registration is a long-drawn-out process and may take decades before benefits of the change-over actually reach the people. In view of the efforts involved in changing over to the new system, there must be a very strong justification for the same. Further, there should be a fair amount of certainty that change would lead to intended results. An objective analysis of the whole issue has been attempted in this chapter to reach a conclusion whether it will be prudent or not for India to go for such a big change.

Any major change in the law of a country has widespread repercussions. This is true about registration law in India also. If India adopts title registration, many changes will be required in the legal and administrative structure relating to land registration. It is important to identify these issues so that the effort involved in going in for the new system is well appreciated before taking policy decisions in this matter. Some of such issues have been discussed in the following paragraphs.

Effect of Title Registration on Substantive Law on Property

Some writers hold the view that registration of title is only a procedural law which provides only a system of keeping records and it is not a new substantive law.[4] The Department of Land Resources appears to hold similar views because a Land Title Bill is proposed to be enacted without much change in the substantive law on property. This view was also taken in England at the time of introduction of title registration. The Land Registry Act, 1862 did not aim at altering the substantive land law. However, it was soon realised that registration cannot be successful unless radical changes are made in the substantial property law. This was done in 1925 by enacting as many as seven legislations together making sweeping changes in the English property law. As far as Australia is concerned, Sir Robert Torrens has himself written that he introduced the Real Property Act in South Australia to 'escape from the grievous yoke of the English Property Law'.[5]

Actually, title registration seeks to introduce new legal principles pertaining to the creation, transaction, registration and enforcement of rights in the property which are bound to affect the existing law on property under the deed registration system. But for these new legal principles, the sanctity of the register, which is the hallmark of title registration, cannot be maintained. Therefore, a country like India having more than a century-old statute law on property with a huge body of related case laws and a well-established system of registering deeds, will have to be prepared for making significant changes in the substantive law on property without which registration of title cannot be implemented. While making changes in the substantive law to implement the registration of title, many legal and administrative issues will have to be resolved first. These issues have been discussed in subsequent paragraphs.

Numerus Clausus Principle

One of the principles of a title registration system as laid down by Ruoff is the 'mirror principle' which means that the register of title always reflects the correct legal situation about the rights over the property. The essence of the 'mirror principle' is that all the rights relating to a property are recorded in the register and nothing exists beyond it. To ensure compliance of this principle, the law on registration of title has to specify the interests that can be registered in the register. The register will not be a true mirror if people are free to create various kinds of interests in land which are not recordable. German real property law follows principle of *numerus clausus* which means that content of rights in property cannot be left to the discretion of the parties involved in the transaction but they have to select from a pool of rights provided in the law.[6] This principle is followed in many other European countries also. However, in India, at present there is no explicit recognition of this principle which is essential for the success of registration of title. On the contrary, in India the Transfer of Property Act allows conditional transfers creating certain future rights which are not discernible at the time of transaction and therefore cannot be registered easily.[7]

Indefeasibility of Registered Title

In the title registration system, a registered title is often called 'indefeasible' which means that no other evidence except the title register can affect the title of a registered owner. However, indefeasibility depends on the specific provisions of the law enacted by the legislature. Different countries have different provisions in this regard.

Static Security of Title

In a deed registration system, the title of an owner cannot be transferred except with his consent. Suppose a conveyance deed in respect of the property of AA is got executed by BB in his favour by fraud, misrepresentation of facts, or any other void means, without the consent of AA, and BB subsequently transfers this property in favour of CC. The transaction in favour of BB is void in the eyes of the law because it was done without the consent of AA. Further transaction by BB in favour of CC is also void because BB was not the real owner at the time of the transfer and therefore was not competent to transfer the property. In this case, AA can retrieve his property from CC through legal process and CC, despite being a bonafide purchaser, has no protection under the deed registration system. This concept, where the title of the real owner is protected under the law and he cannot be deprived of his property except by his consent, is called security of title or static security. This law generally prevails in all the countries until it is modified by the title registration law.

Dynamic Security of Title

Title registration law introduces a new legal principle which provides security of transaction to a bonafide purchaser who has purchased the property on the basis of an entry in the title register. His title is protected against an unregistered claimant, even if the latter is the real owner of the property. Taking the same example as given earlier, if the title of property of AA is registered in the name of BB without the consent of AA and CC buys from BB on the basis of entries in the register of titles, AA cannot retrieve his property because title registration law protects a registered owner and a bonafide purchaser. AA can claim monetary compensation from the Assurance Fund but cannot get back his property. This concept is called security of transaction or dynamic security of title which is the defining characteristic of any title registration law. In Australia, title registration laws offer full protection to a bonafide purchaser and therefore are heavily inclined towards dynamic security of title. However in the English law of title registration, static security to a genuine owner is ensured to a very large extent.

As described in the previous paragraph, dynamic security is an essential feature of title registration law. It actually means that the title of a registered owner is indefeasible even if it is acquired from a person who did not have a good title. This concept has the effect of depriving a genuine owner of his property if his name does not appear in the register. This is a clear injustice to the real owner of the property who is deprived of his property by operation of law for no fault of his.

Deferred Indefeasibility

To balance dynamic and static security, the concept of deferred indefeasibility is used in some of the title registration laws. This concept can be understood with the same example given earlier. If AA detects the inaccuracy in the register before the transfer of property by BB in favour of CC, he may institute legal proceedings to correct the entries in the register and get his property back from BB. However, AA cannot retrieve his property after purchase of the property by CC from BB. In such a case, static security is not affected by the registration of a void transaction but once the property is purchased bonafide by a third person, dynamic security operates and the title of the purchaser is secured. If a law provides immediate indefeasibility, AA cannot retrieve his property from BB also, even if the transfer is through a void transaction.

Protection to Volunteers

The registration laws of England and Australia provide protection of indefeasibility of title only to the purchaser for value. People getting property by way of gift or inheritance, called volunteers, are not protected. However, in Germany, all the registered right holders are protected irrespective of the mode of acquisition of their right. This is one of the issues on which a clear stand has to be taken by a country at the time of introduction of title registration.

Balance between Static and Dynamic Security of Title

While dynamic security is an essential characteristic of a title registration law, it may operate to deprive a genuine owner of his property without any fault of his. A country, while designing a title registration system, has to decide where to strike a balance between static security and dynamic security and draft its title registration law accordingly. In Australia, title registration laws have strong provisions to protect an entry in the title register and courts have interpreted that these laws provide immediate indefeasibility.[8] In English law, the provisions are interpreted to be in favour of differed indefeasibility. In certain circumstances, the English courts have protected the title of the real owner by restoring his property even from a bonafide buyer. If title registration is to be introduced in India, it has to be first decided what kind of static and dynamic security of title is to be provided in the title registration law. The substantive law on property will also require amendments to bring it in coherence with the title registration law.

Indemnity

Ideally, the title register should always reflect the correct legal situation about the rights in the property but this is not the case always as discussed in the previous paragraphs. In many cases, a person not entitled to a right may be able to get registration, and a true right holder may be deprived of his right due to a variety of reasons. The 'curtain principle' of title registration dictates that whatever is written in the register is presumed to be the correct legal position. Due to the operation of new legal principles introduced by the title registration system, some true right holders may be deprived of their rights. To compensate them, some of the countries have an indemnity provision in their title registration law. However, there are many other countries where the title registration system has been implemented without any provision for indemnity from the state. There is no provision of indemnity in the title registration law of Germany and many other countries of continental Europe. Malaysia, Thailand, Fiji and Sudan also do not have such a provision. Also, the law has to lay down the circumstances under which a claim for compensation can be entertained and also whether a claim would be decided by the registrar or the civil courts. Some countries like the Philippines and Hong Kong[9] have provided a maximum ceiling on compensation.

'First Resort' and 'Last Resort' Models

While designing indemnity provisions in the law, there are some choices to be made. In some countries, compensation is payable as a last resort basis while in others it is allowed to be paid as the first resort. In about half of the states of Australia, the 'last resort' model is practised where an aggrieved person gets compensation from the Assurance Fund only if it is not possible to recover his loss from the defaulter through court proceedings. The aggrieved person has to file a case in the appropriate court for compensation against the persons at fault. If compensation cannot be recovered from the defaulter due to his death, bankruptcy or any other reason, the court may order its payment from the Assurance Fund. In the provinces of Western Canada and in the whole of the USA this model is in operation.[10] The law on indemnity in England is more liberal and provides compensation much faster.

Resources for Indemnity Fund

Another issue is the source of funding of the indemnity. In Australia, it is funded by a small levy collected at the time of registration while in England funds are provided from the government budget. At the time of setting up of an indemnity fund, a careful assessment of likely claims has to be made to avoid future problems regarding claims. In 1937, the entire indemnity fund of California State went bankrupt due to a single claim ordered by the court after seventeen years of litigation.[11]

Over-riding Interests

There is another feature of the title registration system which makes compromises on the 'mirror principle' as laid down by Ruoff. Theoretically, all the interests in a property should be recorded in the title register and nothing should exist outside it. However, in practice, all the interests are not recorded in the register and there are certain interests which a buyer has to discover and take appropriate action to protect himself from any adverse impact of those unregistered interests. The registration law does not provide any guarantee or indemnity against these interests which are generally called 'over-riding interests', as these over-ride the entries in the title register. The existence of these interests, in a way, is the measure of discord between the general law on property and the title registration law which no country has been able to eliminate completely.

England has been trying to reduce over-riding interests since 1925 when major changes were effected in the property law there. However, the Land Registration Act, 2002 still has a long list of over-riding interests. In Australia also there are many interests, sometimes called subsisting interests, which affect the rights of a prospective buyer but are not recorded in the register. If India goes in for title registration, it has to decide what type of interests will be recorded in the register and what will be left to be enforced as over-riding interests. If over-riding interests are ignored completely, it will be unfair to people holding those interests, while too many over-riding interests would compromise the integrity of the register and take away the benefits of introducing title registration law.

First Registration

The most crucial part of implementation of a title registration system is bringing all the properties on the title register for the first time. At the time of first registration, the registrar has to examine in detail all the documents forming the basis of title claimed by the applicant. This examination has to be quick but legally sound to generate faith of people in the system. In fact, the registrar has to do the job which is normally performed by a professionally qualified attorney for his client in a deed registration system. Examination of all the documents relating to title at the time of every transaction places enormous powers in the hands of the registrar. There is grave danger of these powers being used either inefficiently or dishonestly by some officials. In both cases, the public will suffer. Another issue is that until all the titles are converted to the new system, a dual system will have to be operated. Looking into the experience of other countries, the time of conversion is very long. Maintenance of a dual system for so long will take away many of the expected outcomes of the title registration system.

First Registration in Australia

This problem was not faced by Australia because title registration was made applicable only to the Crown grants made after the enactment of the new law. First registration was done on the basis of Crown grants which did not require any legal examination. For lands granted earlier than the new law, called general law lands, registration was made optional. Due to this arrangement, the implementation of the new law did not pose any problem in Australia except that general law land could not be brought on the title register for more than a century and a separate deed registration register was maintained for them.

First Registration in England

In England, registration was optional in the beginning under the law in 1862 and 1875 which resulted in almost no registration. Later, registration was made compulsory at the time of the next transaction. However, compulsory registration was extended to more and more counties gradually. It was in 1990 that registration could be made compulsory throughout England and Wales. In England registration is made by the registrar relying mostly on the reports of the qualified advocate of the applicant. It is said that

England could handle the registration because the registrar did not make a detailed examination thinking that any mistakes would be compensated from the indemnity fund. Such a pragmatic approach may not be possible in India.

Rectification of the Title Register

The title registration system is based on the premise that an entry in the register of title is conclusive proof of title. If this is so, there should be no necessity to rectify an existing entry. However, in practice, there are many circumstances under which a wrong entry finds a place in the register and a genuine right holder is deprived of his right without any fault of his. This may be due to a genuine mistake of the registrar or a fraud played by some person. Though the indemnity provision compensates the genuine owner in such cases there are cases where justice demands restoring the property to the genuine right holder. This can be done only by rectification of the title register. Different countries have different provisions in this regard. In Australia, the register is rectified in very rare cases and that too on the orders of a civil court. The civil courts also generally maintain the sanctity of the register and do not interfere often. However, in England, the registrar is empowered to rectify the register to correct mistakes and restore the property to the genuine right holder. Indemnity is provided to that person who suffers because of this rectification. In Germany, the register is not corrected by the registrar but the parties are advised to settle the dispute through the civil court. So while introducing title registration in a country, there has to be a conscious decision regarding the degree of affirmation to be provided to the register and accordingly provision of rectification is to be drafted.

Boundary and Cadastre

The role of cadastre (record-of-rights) in the new regime of title registration has to be drafted carefully. Australia and England did not face this issue because there was no cadastre there and rights were recorded by the registrar with reference to individual maps of property submitted at the time of registration. In England, ordinance maps are used as index maps to fix the location of the property but boundaries are not accurately defined. In Germany, works relating to cadastre and registration are dealt with by different agencies. Accurate cadastral maps are available with the cadastral authorities and all the registration is done with reference to those maps. However, the registration authority keeps a copy of the cadastre in the form of the first part of the Land Register in which rights are recorded. In respect of rights of people, the record of the registrar is considered final while in respect of measurements and other cadastral features of property, the record of the cadastral authority is final. In India, there is a tradition of making a detailed cadastre and mediating boundary disputes between land owners. This role of government authorities may have to be reviewed under the new law.

Merger of Cadastre and Registration Offices

At present, maintenance of cadastre, called record-of-rights in India, and deed registration are handled by different agencies. The National Land Records Modernization Programme envisages the merger of these two functions in a single agency. So the work of maintaining the cadastre is either to be transferred to the present registrars or the revenue officers responsible for maintaining record-of-rights are to be entrusted with the registration also. Either of these options will be a huge challenge for state governments. Presently, deed registration is done by sub-registrars deputed at district and sub-district level who are exclusively entrusted with this work only. However, these sub-registrars do not have any field staff in their organisation and therefore cannot handle regular updating of record-of-rights which involves field inspection, survey and many other such operations. On the other hand, the revenue officers, i.e. Collector, *Tehsildar*, Sub-divisional Magistrate, etc., have been entrusted with many other works of general administration like law and order, disaster management, community development, etc. They are hardly capable of handling the additional work of registration which requires continuous engagement for quick service to the people.

Registration of Hereditary Rights

The experience with the system of deed registration and record-of-rights in India demonstrates that hereditary rights are a major source of litigation in India. This is so because succession laws are complex in India and it is very difficult to determine with certainty the hereditary rights of a person at the time of making an entry in the record-of-rights. The same problem is faced by a buyer of an ancestral property in finding out whether there are claimants other than the seller. Because of the nature of succession law in India, this problem will remain even if a title registration system is adopted in the country. In a title registration system, the rights of the people have to be accurately recorded in the title register which means that the registrar has to decide on the rights of the successors at the time of registration of inheritance due to the death of a person. Looking into the complexity of succession laws in India, this will be hard task for the registrar. Some peculiar characteristics of succession law in India are listed below to highlight the complexity of the issue.

(i) The law on intestate succession for different communities in India is governed by different succession laws applicable for that particular community, viz., the Hindu Succession Act, Indian Succession Act, Shariat laws, etc.

(ii) The law on succession by will is governed by the Indian Succession Act, 1925 for all communities except Muslims. The law in relation to making of wills by Muslims is governed by the relevant Muslim Shariat Law as applicable to Shias and Sunnis. However, within the State of West Bengal and within the jurisdiction of the Madras and Bombay High Courts, the Indian Succession Act is applicable to wills made by Muslims also.

(iii) Hindu law is divided into two schools, the Dayabhaga and Mitakshara. Dayabhaga prevails in West Bengal, Assam,

Tripura and in most parts of Odisha whereas Mitakshara is followed in the rest of India. Mitakshara law is again divided into Benaras, Mithila, Mayukha (Bombay) and Dravida (Southern) sub-schools.

(iv) Under Dayabhaga, the father is regarded as the absolute owner of his property, whether it is self-acquired or inherited from his ancestors.

(v) Mitakshara law draws a distinction between ancestral property (also referred to as joint family property or co-parcenary property) and separate (e.g., property inherited from mother) and self-acquired properties. All the children are joint owners of the ancestral property along with their father even during his lifetime. In other words, a child acquires the right in an ancestral property at his birth itself. It is almost impossible to keep track of the owners of ancestral property because with every new birth in the family, the number of owners and their shares change.

Change-over to Title Registration Not Advisable

All the relevant aspects of land registration in India and other countries have hitherto been discussed. The following evidence emerges from the facts and analysis in this regard.

1. The main problems in the present land registration system in India are poorly updated land records especially in urban areas, heavy litigation, difficulty in assessing the encumbrance on land at the time of purchase and an inefficient delivery system. These problems are mostly related to poor implementation of existing laws and therefore a complete change-over to a new system is not required.

2. There is no evidence that pendency of a large number of cases relating to land disputes is caused because of the deed registration system in India. It also not certain that pendency of land-related disputes will reduce by implementation of the title registration system in India.

3. Among the top ten economies of the world, the USA, Japan, Italy, France, India and Brazil have deed registration systems; Germany and the United Kingdom have title registration; Canada follows both systems and China is in the process of implementing a title registration system. Thus, both the systems have a widespread following in the world and there are examples of very successful land markets under both the systems.

4. A large number of developed countries in the world are using the deed registration system successfully. They, however, have made certain improvements in the basic deed registration as per their specific requirements. The USA has introduced Title Insurance through private companies; France has provided 'Real Estate File' and the Netherlands has made certain changes in the law to give protection to a bonafide buyer. India can also reform the existing system without going altogether for a new system.

5. The title registration system appears to be superior to the deed registration system because the concept of the conclusiveness of a registered title in the former. However, in practice, there are many limitations on the conclusiveness of title in the title registration system. Experience has shown that in none of the title registration systems is the title register absolutely conclusive. There are always some exceptions to the conclusiveness of the registered title in every title registration law.

6. In the title registration system, getting a claim from the indemnity fund is not as simple as it appears to be. An owner losing his land without any fault of his has to go through litigation in the civil court to get compensation from the government.

7. Title registration does not provide perfect security of title. Due to this reason title insurance through private companies is very common even in those areas of the USA where title registration is followed. The title insurance business is increasing in Canada and Australia also.

8. Title registration system has a mixed record of success around the world. The USA has tried to introduce title registration but had to revert back to deed registration finally. Title registration has failed in most parts of Latin America also. Hong Kong has passed the title registration law in 2004 but its implementation has been kept in abeyance due to objections by the Bills Committee of the Legislative Council.

9. Title registration law introduces a new legal principle which provides security of transaction to a bonafide purchaser who has purchased a property on the basis of an entry in the title register. His title is protected against an unregistered claimant, even if the latter is the real owner of the property. It actually means that the title of a registered owner is indefeasible even if it is acquired from a person who did not have a good title. This concept has the effect of depriving a genuine owner of his property if his name does not appear in the register due to a fraud or mistake. This is a clear injustice to the real owner of the property who is deprived of his property without any fault of his.

10. Introduction of the title registration system in India will require wide-ranging changes in the present legal principles. The central and state governments will have to amend many existing laws and enact new ones to implement title registration. Such wide-ranging changes in the law will involve huge effort on the part of the central and state governments.

11. The most crucial part of implementation of the title registration system is bringing all the properties on the title register for the first time. At the time of first registration, the registrar has to examine in detail all the documents forming the basis of the title claimed by the applicant. In fact, the registrar has to do a job which is normally performed by a professionally qualified attorney in a deed registration system. The examination of all the documents relating to a title at the time of every transaction will place

enormous powers in the hands of the registrar. There is a danger of some officials using these powers either inefficiently or dishonestly. In both the situations, the public will suffer.

12. In India we have a very long history of land rights and it will be very difficult to investigate the title at the time of first registration. In Australia, title registration was introduced very early in its history when grants of land to settlers had just begun. Moreover, title registration was made applicable to land grants issued subsequent to the new law only. Therefore, they never faced the situation of investigating very old titles over land.

13. The experience with the system of deed registration and record-of-rights in India demonstrates that hereditary rights are a major source of litigation. This is so because succession laws are very complex in India. Because of the nature of succession laws this problem will remain even if the title registration system is adopted.

14. In case of introduction of title registration in India, a dual system will have to be operated until all the titles are converted to the new system. Looking at the experience of other countries, the time of conversion is very long. Maintenance of a dual system for a long period will take away many of the expected outcomes of the title registration system.

In view of the above facts, it is not advisable that India change over to the title registration system from the present deed registration system. The present problems relating to land registration are not likely to be solved by a change in the system. Rather, such a change may invite more administrative and legal problems. Instead of wasting its effort in experimenting with an alien system, India should reform its deed registration system as has been done by many other countries. The advantages of reforming the present system is that incremental improvements can be made in it. The effect of such improvements will be visible early and corrective measures can be taken if something does not work out as expected.

NOTES

1. (National Commission to Review the Working of the Constitution 2002) (National Commission to Review the Working of the Constitution 2002)
2. (The National Land Records Modernization Programme, Guidelines, Technical Manuals and MIS 2008-09)
3. (PRS Legislative Research)
4. (Simpson 1976) p. 168
5. (Torrens 1859) p. 44
6. (Wilsch 2012) p. 226
7. (The Transfer of Property Act, 1882) Secs. 25-34
8. (O'Connor, Deferred and Immediate Indefeasibility: Bijural Ambiguity in Registered Land Title Systems 2009) p. 203
9. Title registration law has been enacted but has not yet been implemented in Hong Kong.
10. (O'Connor, The Top 10 Legal Questions for Registered Title Systems 2010) p. 12
11. (Simpson 1976) p. 180

CHAPTER 8

Recommendations for Improvement in Land Registration in India

In the last chapter it was established that it is not appropriate for India to venture into the new territory of the title registration system. Instead, it should direct its efforts and financial resources to make improvements in the present system. The Indian deed registration system together with record-of-rights has many points of strength on which an efficient registration system can be built. While documents relating to transfer of rights in the property are registered with the registrar under the Registration Act, 1908, land parcel-wise ownership records and cadastral maps are maintained by the revenue departments in each state. These two systems are more or less working independently with a very weak link between them. Therefore, in addition to making improvements in these two systems separately, legal provisions are to be made to link both of them so that synergy between them can be utilized. Some improvements in the present system are recommended in the following paragraphs.

Proof of Ownership at the Time of Registration

The present deed registration system can be made more reliable if the registrar is allowed to verify prima facie the ownership of the transferor. As per sec. 7 of the Transfer of Property Act, only the owner is competent to transfer a right in the property. However, under the Registration Act, the registrar, at the time of registration of a transfer deed, does not have the mandate to examine the competence of the transferor to transfer the property. It is entirely the responsibility of the transferee to verify the competence of the transferor. The present deed system can be made more reliable if the registrar is assigned the duty of prima facie verification of the title of the transferor.

Prima facie proof of title of the transferor will be taken care of if attachment of a copy of the record-of-rights and cadastral map with the deed is made compulsory under the law. A deed should be accepted for registration only when the name of the transferor appears in the record-of-rights. In case his name does not appear there, he should be advised to get his name recorded in the record-of-rights before registering the deed of transfer. If, in certain areas, it is not possible to attach copies of record-of-rights, the concerned state government may prescribe any other record to be attached with the deed as proof of title.

However, the registrar should not be given excessive powers to go into the merits of the title of the transferor and reject the registration on this basis. He should only ensure that the prescribed documents are attached with the deed and the title of the transferor is recorded in them. This provision will make a huge improvement in the system and reduce future litigations.

While making this change in the law, the Netherlands pattern may be followed. In the Netherlands, the registrar has been authorized to inform the parties if he thinks that the transferor does not have a valid title or is not authorised to transfer the property.[1] In such cases, the notary normally withdraws the deed submitted by him on behalf of his client. In the unlikely event of the parties insisting on transfer of such deed, the registrar is obliged to register it.

This change will help in updating the record-of-rights on a regular basis. At present, a person acquiring a right in an immovable property is legally bound to inform the prescribed authority for making changes in the record-of-rights. The law provides for imposition of a penalty in case of failure of a person to inform the authority but this provision is seldom enforced. Due to this reason, many a time a person does not report to the authority and entries in the record-of-rights are not updated. With this change in the law, an owner would have to get his ownership recorded in the record-of-rights without which he will not be able sell his property in the future.

Description of Property in the Transfer Deed

Another aspect where the record-of-rights and the deed registry have to be linked is the description of the property in the deed presented for registration. The exact description of the property mentioned in the deed with reference to the record-of-rights should be made compulsory to avoid future litigation.

The present provisions in secs. 21 and 22 of the Registration Act, 1908 read as follows:

"21. Description of property and maps or plans.

(1) No non-testamentary document relating to immovable property shall be accepted for registration unless it contains a description of such property sufficient to identify the same.

(2) Houses in towns shall be described as situate on the north or other side of the street or road (which should be specified) to which they front, and by their existing and former occupancies, and by their numbers if the houses in such street or road are numbered.

(3) Other houses and land shall be described by their name, if any, and as being the territorial division in which they are situate, and by their superficial contents, the roads and other properties on which they abut, and their existing occupancies, and also, whenever it is practicable, by reference to a government map or survey.

(4) No non-testamentary document containing a map or plan of any property comprised therein shall be accepted for registration unless it is accompanied by a true copy of the map

or plan, or, in case such property is situate in several districts, by such number of true copies of the map or plans as are equal to the number of such districts.

22. Description of houses and land by reference to government maps of surveys.

(1) Where it is, in the opinion of the State Government, practicable to describe houses, not being houses in towns, and lands by reference to a government map or survey, the State Government may, by rule made under this Act, require that such houses and lands as aforesaid shall, for the purposes of section 21, be so described.

(2) Save as otherwise provided by any rule made under sub-section (1), failure to comply with the provisions of section 21, sub-section (2) or sub-section (3), shall not disentitle a document to be registered if the description of the property to which it relates is sufficient to identify that property."

It is mentioned here that wherever possible, property should be described with reference to the government map or survey but description with respect to government map or survey has not been made mandatory. It has been left to the state governments to make it mandatory by making rules in this regard under sec. 22(1).

This leaves the description of property to the discretion of the parties. In most of the cases, especially in urban areas, it is described by the name of the properties or other structures located on its boundaries without a precise map of the property. This description, most often, is not supported by any government record, survey or map. This practice makes the resolution of future disputes regarding dimension and boundaries of the property very difficult and parties have to go for long-drawn litigation. A registered deed is not only an agreement between the two parties but is also a notice to third parties. Therefore, the description of property has to be such that it can be understood by a third party also. It cannot be left to the wisdom and discretion of the parties to the deed alone. The law has to intervene to prescribe the form and manner of such description.

Some states have made certain amendments in the Registration Act providing for better description of property in the transfer deeds. Maharashtra and Gujarat have amended Sec. 21 (2) and provided that 'In all city surveyed areas, houses and lands shall also be described by their cadastral survey numbers.' These states have also amended sec.22 (2) to make the description of the property by cadastral numbers compulsory in the city surveyed areas.[2]

Recommendation of the Law Commission

The Law Commission of India has recommended the following provisions regarding description of property:

(i) 'Houses and lands in Municipal areas shall be described by the area, boundaries, municipal town survey number, the municipal door number, if any, and whenever it is practicable, by reference to government map or survey.

(ii) In all other places, houses and lands shall be described by their area, boundaries, survey number or *paimaish* or other like number, if any, and, whenever it is practicable, by reference to a Government map or survey.'[3]

It is recommended that both in urban and rural areas, the description of property with reference to the record-of-rights and the cadastral map and attachment of copies thereof should be made mandatory by amending secs. 21 and 22 of the Registration Act. This will also satisfy the requirement of proof of ownership as recommended earlier. In those areas where authentic cadastral maps do not exist, the transferor should get a special survey of the piece of property proposed to be transferred, done by the concerned government officials or approved private surveyor and attach the copies with the deed. In this survey, location and dimensions of the property will be accurately marked with reference to nearby properties and permanent landmarks. A similar practice is followed in Australia where, at the time of registration of transfer of property, stand-alone survey maps are attached with the transfer documents.

Transfer of Part of Property

Another related issue is the procedure in case of transfer of a part of the property. It should be provided in the law that a sale deed in respect of a part of the property will not be registered unless a new map showing a clear division of the property between the seller and purchaser is attached with the sale deed. As per the present practice in such cases, part of the property is described by its physical features and in terms of share of the whole property without defining the exact boundaries and measurements. However, later, disputes are created when the transferee goes to get his ownership recorded in the record-of-rights. In the record-of-rights, the ownership of the new owner of a part of property cannot be recorded unless the land is partitioned as per the procedure laid down in the relevant law of the state and new maps are prepared for the land so partitioned. To shorten this procedure, sometimes the transferee is recorded as a shareholder in the whole property but in that case he does not get ownership right over a specific piece of land. This situation is a potential source of litigation in land transactions.

To prevent this situation, attachment of a new map showing a clear division between the seller and purchaser should be made mandatory. This map should be approved by the authority responsible for making the cadastral map in the state so that later on there is no objection in making entries in the record-of-rights as per this map.

The sale of his share by one of the owners in a joint property also leads to disputes later. In such cases, even if seller gives possession of a part of the property, the buyer does not have absolute claim on the ownership of his possession. He just steps into shoes of the seller and becomes a shareholder in the joint property. He gets absolute ownership of his share only after the formal partition. To prevent such types of disputes, one of the shareholders in a joint property should not be allowed to sell his share unless a formal partition is done as per law and the boundaries of his share are clearly demarcated. This procedure is followed in the title registration systems of Australia, England and Germany and also in the deed registration system of France.

Compulsory Registration of All Transactions

Under the Registration Act, 1908, a large number of documents are exempted from registration. Due to these exemptions, many documents which affect the rights in a property do not appear in the record of the registry. In a title registration system, all the rights are compulsorily registered in the title register and therefore a prospective buyer can know the correct state of rights and interests in the property (with some exceptions) from the title register. To achieve this position in India, all the exemptions from registration of documents affecting rights in the property should be withdrawn.

Right in property is considered *'jus in rem'*, i.e., right enforceable against the world at large. Thus, the very nature of a right in the land requires that there should be a notice to the world at large about any change in the rights held in a property. The registration of a deed has the effect of giving notice to third parties about the new acquisition of rights in that property. Therefore, all the transactions in the property must be registered without any exemption so that the records of the registrar reflect the true status of rights in the property.

In India, it is compulsory to register most of the transactions in the immovable property. It is clearly provided in sec. 49 of the Registration Act that a document which is required to be registered under the Transfer of Property Act or under the Registration Act shall not affect any immovable property and shall not be received as evidence of any transaction affecting that property unless it is duly registered. However, this strict stance of Indian law in favour of registration gets diluted by exempting a large number of documents from registration and making registration optional for certain documents. Due to these exemptions, many documents which affect rights in the property do not appear in the record of the registry and it is almost impossible for a prospective buyer or a mortgagee to discover the rights created by these documents.

The necessity of removing these exemptions has been emphasised by many experts. Justice K. Kanan[4] has observed 'we need to probably move towards compulsory registration for many more documents as well, such as all types of family settlement or family partition, wills, leases and equitable mortgages, if we must decongest courts from certain types of litigation involving these documents.'[5]

Recommendation of Law Commission

The first Law Commission of India headed by a legal luminary, M. C. Setalvad, examined the Registration Act in 1908 in detail and gave its recommendation in its sixth report. It has observed, 'We consider that time has come for removing the exemption in respect of instruments where the value of right, title or interest dealt with is below one hundred rupees.'[6] To this effect, it has recommended some changes in sec. 17(1)(b)[7] and also in the Transfer of Property Act, 1882[8]. The Law Commission also recommended the removal of exemption for composition deeds as provided in sec. 17(2)(i).[9] It further recommended that instead of exempting an order of a public officer and decree of the court as is done under sec. 17(2), these authorities should be required to send a copy of such order and decree to the registrar who should file them in Book No. 1. The Law Commission recommended widening the scope of sec. 89 to include all the orders of public officers and courts which are otherwise exempted from registration under sec. 17(2). Going further, it recommended that information about all the admitted plaints and memorandum of appeals relating to immovable property should be sent by the court to the concerned sub-registrar who will place them in Book No. 1.[10]

Thus, all transactions, documents, decrees, orders, etc., affecting the rights in immovable property should either be registered or information about them be sent to the registrar for filing in Book

No. 1. This single measure will greatly increase the reliability of records of the registry resulting in reduced disputes related to property. The recommendations made by the Law Commission in its sixth report can be taken as the basis for making changes in the relevant laws.

Record of Pending Litigation

In India, there is no way of knowing about any pending litigation in relation to a property by a prospective buyer. This situation is a major source of litigation in the sale and purchase of a property. There is a need to make amendments in the Registration Act, 1908 providing for registration of notice of a pending litigation.

Under a deed registration system, the grantor can transfer only those rights which are held by him at the time of transfer following the maxim *'Nemo dat quod non habet'*, meaning "no one gives what he doesn't have." A transfer would be invalid, even if made through a valid registered deed, if a court by a subsequent order holds that the grantor did not have the right to transfer that property. To ensure justice to the litigant parties, it is necessary to maintain the status quo till the court finally decides the rights of each party. Sec. 52 of the Transfer of Property Act, 1882 provides that,

> '...the property cannot be transferred or otherwise dealt with by any party to the suit or proceeding so as to affect the rights of any other party thereto under any decree or order which may be made therein, except under the authority of the court and on such terms as it may impose.'

This is called the principle of *'Pendente lite nihil innovetur'* meaning 'during litigation, nothing should be changed.' Under this provision, the sale of a property under litigation is not prevented but the rights of a grantee are subject to the final decision of the court. If the rights of the grantor are curtailed by the court order, the rights of the grantee would also be curtailed to the same extent.

In view of this legal position, it is necessary that a buyer knows

RECOMMENDATIONS FOR IMPROVEMENT IN LAND REGISTRATION IN INDIA

about the pending litigation relating to a property so that he can take a well-informed decision regarding his purchase. At present, there is no provision for the recording of the position of pending litigation either in the deed registry or in the record-of-rights.

Recommendation of the Supreme Court

The gravity of the matter has been recognised by the highest court of the country that has suggested the enactment of a suitable law to correct this situation. The observation of the Supreme Court in T. G. Ashok Kumar vs. Govindammal & Others[11] is quoted below:

> '...At present, a prospective purchaser can easily find out about any existing encumbrance over a property either by inspection of the Registration Registers or by securing a certificate relating to encumbrances (that is copies of entries in the Registration Registers) from the jurisdictional Sub-Registrar under Section 57 of the Registration Act, 1908. But a prospective purchaser has no way of ascertaining whether there is any suit or proceeding pending in respect of the property, if the person offering the property for sale does not disclose it or deliberately suppresses the information. ....The *pendente lite* purchaser will have to wait for the litigation to come to an end or he may have to take over the responsibility of conducting the litigation if the transferor loses interest after the sale.... All these inconveniences, risks, hardships and misery could be avoided and the property litigations could be reduced to a considerable extent, if there is some satisfactory and reliable method by which a prospective purchaser can ascertain whether any suit is pending (or whether the property is subject to any decree or attachment) before he decides to purchase the property.

> 'It is of some interest that a solution has been found to this problem in the State of Maharashtra by an appropriate local amendment to section 52 of the Act, by the Bombay Act 4 of 1939.... We hope that the Law Commission and Parliament considers such amendment or other suitable amendment to cover the existing void in title verification or due diligence procedures. Provision can also be made for compulsory

registration of such notices in respect of decrees and in regard to attachments of immovable properties.'

Recommendation of the Law Commission

Interestingly, much before this judgement, in 1998, the Law Commission had deliberated on this issue and suggested amendments in sec. 52 of the Transfer of Property Act, 1882 and secs. 18 & 78 of the Registration Act, 1908 in its 157th report.[12] The Law Commission suggested that notices of pending suits and proceedings be registered under sec. 18 of the Registration Act and protection of sec. 52 of the Transfer of Property Act should be available to the parties only if such notice is duly registered.

In view of the above, provision for registration of notice of pending litigation should be made in the Registration Act, 1908 as per the recommendation of the Law Commission. This will go a long way in reducing land-related litigation.

Compulsory Registration of Wills

Inheritance of property through a Will overriding the normal rules of inheritance is a constant source of litigation in India. At present, it is optional for a testator to register his Will any time after it has been written. The successors of a deceased person also have the option to register the will left by him at any time after his death, or not to register it at all. The law does not give any priority to a registered Will over an unregistered Will. Due to this legal position, sometimes after the death of a person, multiple unregistered Wills appear in the possession of interested parties leading to long-drawn out litigation. This situation can be improved if registration of a will is made compulsory under the law. The Standing Committee of Parliament on Rural Development in its report[13] on Registration (Amendment) Bill 2013 has recommended compulsory registration of Wills.

Therefore, registration of Wills should be made compulsory by making amendments in the Registration Act and the Indian

Succession Act, 1925. In case of a registered will not being available, the property should devolve on the legal heirs as per rules laid down in the relevant law.

Mortgage by Deposit of Deeds

The Transfer of Property Act provides for creation of mortgage on property by simply depositing the title deeds with the lender without registering any kind of deed. In this case, no deed of any kind is required to be registered.[14] This kind of mortgage is also referred to as equitable mortgage. Equitable mortgage is extensively used by financial institutions to advance housing loans because of the simplicity of procedure and saving on the registration fee and stamp duty. However, this provision gives rise to the possibility of fraud by selling the mortgaged property on the basis of forged documents. This provision needs review because such a mortgage does not appear in the records of the registry and therefore there is no notice to a subsequent purchaser or the mortgagee. This is also against the spirit of sec. 17(b) of the Registration Act. The Registration (Amendment) Bill 2013 pending in the *Rajya Sabha* seeks to correct this situation by including an agreement to deposit deeds for equitable mortgage under the category of compulsorily registrable documents and making it mandatory for the financial institution to send information on the sanction of loans on the basis of equitable mortgage to the registrar.

It is recommended that either mortgage by deposit of title deeds should be abolished or a memorandum regarding deposit of title deeds should be registered with the registrar at a nominal fee.

Reducing Gap between Execution and Registration

To ensure that records of the registry reflect the true legal position and to prevent multiple transactions in respect of the same property, registration should be done at the earliest after execution of an instrument. The Registration Act allows four months for registration with the provision of further extension of four months with the permission of the registrar. This is too long a time in today's world of fast communication. During this period, which is termed as 'Registration Gap', there is a possibility of execution of another deed by the grantor hiding the execution of an earlier deed. There is also possibility of filing a suit in a court by a person claiming that property without knowing that it has already been disposed of. In such cases, litigation is bound to take place. Therefore, the time allowed for registration should be reduced to one month. In genuine cases, extension up to one month may be allowed.

Alteration in Record-of-Rights

The first step towards making the record-of-rights reliable is not allowing any alteration in the record except on the application of a right holder or a person claiming to be the right holder. At present, there are provisions in some state laws to initiate amendments in the records by the officials themselves to correct clerical mistakes, to record undisputed changes, to implement orders of revenue officers, to update the record on the basis of information from sources other than a right holder and other similar reasons.[15] These provisions make the record vulnerable to the genuine errors as well as deliberate manipulation by the vested interests. All such provisions should be removed from law or their scope should be severely restricted. For alteration in the records on the basis of an application by the concerned parties, detailed provision as to circumstances under which such application can be entertained and procedure for making such alteration must be incorporated in the law to take away any discretion of officials in this regard. Presently, such detailed provisions are not provided in most of the state laws.

Thus changes in the record-of-rights should be initiated only on the basis of application of a right holder, or a person claiming to be the right holder.

Prompt Disposal of Disputes by Revenue Officers

The biggest strength of the record-of-rights is that it is subject to an adjudication mechanism to resolve any dispute regarding entries made in the record. This mechanism gives an opportunity to people to guard their interests without any need to approach a civil court. In most of the state laws, the civil courts are barred from interfering with disputes pending before a revenue officer regarding making and updating record-of-rights. However, over the years, this adjudication mechanism has also become one of the weaknesses of the record-of-rights.

Provision in the law for multiple appeals, review and revision is the main reason for the huge pendency of cases with revenue officers. Many times these provisions are misused by unscrupulous persons to deliberately prolong the proceedings, which has the effect of denying justice to a genuine right holder. In Maharashtra, two appeals are provided for against any order of the revenue officer in relation to making or updating the record-of-rights. In addition to this, a revenue officer, on the application of any party or on his own motion, can review an order passed by him or his predecessor. Further, the state government may at any time modify, annul or reverse any order passed by any officer.[16] Almost similar provisions are there in the Punjab law also.[17]

At the time of making the record-of-rights for the first time, entries are made on the basis of inspection of each land parcel, evidence of title produced by the right holder and entries in any previous record-of-rights. During the process of making new records, copies of draft entries are provided to all the right holders and record is read over in their presence before final publication. Subsequent updating is done mostly on the basis of some documentary evidence produced before the revenue officer like registered conveyance deed, will, probate order, order for partition, court order, etc. The revenue officer decides what entry is to be made in the record-of-rights based on such documentary evidence. He is not supposed to go into intricate questions of law while taking this decision.

As per general principles of jurisprudence in India, only a civil court can decide the title of a person conclusively. Therefore, any number of appeals before a revenue officer will not settle a legal dispute relating to a title for which a claimant has to finally go to a civil court. As entries in the record-of-rights are not conclusive proof of title, there is no need of providing for multiple appeals and further provisions for review and revision.

In West Bengal and Karnataka, only one appeal has been provided for and there is no provision for review or revision of orders either on an application of a party or on the motion of the revenue officer. This pattern should be followed by other states also to avoid prolonged litigation resulting in uncertainty to the entries in the record-of-rights.

Reducing Gap between Acquisition of Right and Entry in Record-of-Rights

As recommended earlier, in the case of registration of deeds, there is also a need to reduce the gap between acquisition of a right and entry of that right in the record-of-rights. Many times, record-of-rights is not updated for a long time and therefore does not reflect the correct position of legal rights. Under the Land Revenue Acts of the states, it is mandatory for every person to inform about his acquisition of a right within three months to the revenue official. There is a provision of a small penalty also in case of failure to inform such acquisition. However, there is no adverse consequence to a person if he fails to give such information in time. The revenue officer enters the mutation on delayed information also and penalty is seldom imposed.

This situation can be corrected to a large extent by a few changes in the law regarding record-of-rights. First, time for reporting about acquisition of a right should be reduced to one month from the present three months. Second, a graded and sufficiently steep mutation fee structure, linked to delay in reporting, may be prescribed to deter people from late reporting of transactions. Finally, it should be provided in the law that if a person fails to report acquisition of right within the prescribed time and in the meantime some other person gets the same right recorded in his favour on the basis of valid documents and within the prescribed time, the revenue officer will not entertain the application of the former for correction of records. He, however, may go to a civil court for declaration of his right.

Record of Intestate Succession

It has been experienced that hereditary rights are a major source of litigation in India. This is so because succession laws are very complex in this country. The law on succession for different communities in India is governed by different succession laws, viz., the Hindu Succession Act, Indian Succession Act, Shariat laws, etc.

One of the peculiarities of Hindu succession law is the distinction between ancestral property and self-acquired property in the ownership of the same person. While he has full rights to dispose of his self-acquired property, his rights to alienate the ancestral property are severely limited by the law. Any alienation of the ancestral property by him in violation of the law can be disputed by other coparceners at a later stage affecting the title of a bonafide purchaser. Rules for succession are also different in respect of two types of properties. However, in the record-of-rights only the name of the person holding the land is recorded without mentioning whether it is his self-acquired property or the ancestral property. Therefore, a prospective buyer cannot easily know the limitation on the right of holder to alienate the property.

To avoid this situation, respective state laws should provide for a separate folio for self-acquired property and ancestral property. Any limitation on the right of the owner to dispose of his property should also be mentioned in the record-of-rights.

Recording Objections in Record-of-Rights

There may be certain circumstances in which a person has genuine objection to transfer of a property. This may be in case of mutation on the basis of an objectionable will, transfer by inheritance in violation of law, transfer ignoring pre-emption rights, etc. At present, there is no provision in the law to record such objections. The only option before an aggrieved person is to acquire an injunction from a civil court to stop such transaction.

To avoid unnecessary litigation, a provision should be made in the law to record objections in the record-of-rights on the basis of an application by a person claiming a right in the property. In the case of such objections, three month's time may be given to the applicant to bring an order of the competent court. If he fails to bring such an order, objection should be removed from the records. Such provision exists in the German law.

Applicability of Transfer of Property Act for All Religions

As per sec 2, nothing in chapter II of the Act 'shall be deemed to affect any rule of Mohammedan law.' Transfer of immovable property creates *'jus in rem'*, i.e., right enforceable against anyone in the world and therefore it should be based on the principles explicitly laid down in the law which can be understood by everyone. Chapter II of the Act contains important principles regarding transfer of property like what can be transferred, person competent to transfer, rule against perpetuity, conditional transfer, transfer by co-owner, etc., and making these provisions subject to Mohammedan law, which is largely un-codified, is bound to create uncertainty about the validity of a transaction especially when parties to the transfer may be from different religions.

Therefore, either the Transfer of Property Act should be made universally applicable or the rules of Mohammedan law affecting the provisions of this Act should be mentioned in the Act itself.

Applicability of Transfer of Property Act in Whole of India

As per sec. 1 of the Act, it was not extended to Part B States and States of Bombay, Punjab and Delhi. The concerned state governments have powers to extend this Act or a part thereof to the whole or any part of the state. Since then, many state governments have extended this law or part thereof to their territories but still this law has not been extended to the whole of India. For example, all the provisions of this law have not been extended to all the areas of Delhi and Punjab.

It is recommended that to bring uniformity and remove ambiguity in this regard, this law should be made applicable to the whole of India by an amendment in the Act.

Conditional Transfer of Property

The Transfer of Property Act allows a person to transfer his property either absolutely or conditionally incorporating a salutary principle that the law favours freedom of transfer of property.[18] The owner is allowed to impose any condition on use, transfer and obligations of transferee towards a third party and the like, with the only limitation that it should not restrain 'absolutely' further disposal of property. The concept of imposition of conditions on transfer which includes sale, lease, mortgage and gift (sec. 5), goes against the free alienability of immovable property which is essential for a modern land market. The rules for valid and invalid conditions; whether a condition is required to be fulfilled 'substantially' or 'strictly'; whether the happening of a specified uncertain event is impossible and other such related matters are not amenable to easy interpretation leading to prolonged litigation.

Therefore, provisions in the Transfer of Property Act require a thorough review in the context of present day socio-economic requirements.

Transfer by Person Other than Owner

There is another class of provisions in the Act which has the potential to create uncertainty to the title of immovable property, i.e., transfer of property by a person other than the true owner or his agent. These rules contained in secs. 35, 38, 41 and 43 provide that in certain conditions such transfer can be legitimised. These provisions are against the basic law that only the owner of a property has authority to transfer it.

It is recommended that in the interest of certainty to title and free marketability of land, no such contingency should be allowed by law and it should be clearly laid down that all transfers done by an unauthorised person will be void.

Entry in Record-of-Rights as Constructive Notice

Under the Transfer of Property Act, it is provided that a person acquiring a registered immovable property is deemed to have notice of the registered deed in respect of that property. Due to this provision, in case of any dispute in future, he cannot take a plea that he was not aware of earlier transactions. The record-of-rights is also a public document where rights of people are recorded after due inquiry and presumption of truth is attached to this record. It will be appropriate if entries in the record-of-rights are given the same legal status as the record of deed registry.

Therefore, entries in the record-of-rights relating to a particular property should also be considered as deemed notice to any person acquiring that property. An appropriate amendment in the Transfer of Property Act should be made to incorporate this principle.

NOTES

1. (Hendrik Ploeger 2016) p. 14
2. Bombay Act 35 of 1958 and Gujarat Act, 11 of 1960
3. (Law Commission of India 1957), p. 44, Sec. 7 of the draft of amendments in the Registration Act proposed by the Commission.

4. Formerly Judge of the Punjab and Haryana High Court and author of many law books.
5. (Mulla 2016), preface to thirteenth edition
6. (Law Commission of India 1957) p. 12
7. (Law Commission of India 1957) p. 13
8. (Law Commission of India 1957) p. 92
9. (Law Commission of India 1957) p. 17
10. (Law Commission, 1957), p. 58, sec .42 of the draft of amendments in Registration Act proposed by the Commission.
11. T. G. Ashok Kumar v. Govindammal and another, (2011) 2 MLJ 317 (SC)
12. (Law Commission of India 1998)
13. (Standing Committee on Rural Development, Sixteenth Lok Sabha 2015)
14. (The Transfer of Property Act, 1882) Sec. 58(f)
15. (The Punjab Land Revenue Act, 1887) Sec. 34-37, (The Maharashtra Land Revenue Code 1966) Sec. 155, (The West Bengal Land Reforms Act, 1955) Sec. 50A, 51A, 51B, (The Karnataka Land Revenue Act, 1964) Sec. 58
16. (The Maharashtra Land Revenue Code 1966) Secs. 246-259
17. (The Punjab Land Revenue Act, 1887) Secs. 13-16
18. (The Transfer of Property Act, 1882), Sec. 7

APPENDIX A

Analysis of Laws on Record-of-Rights in Select States

Record-of-Rights in Maharashtra

Preliminary

1. Maharashtra came into existence on 1 May 1960, when the former state of Bombay was split on a linguistic basis into Gujarat and Maharashtra. It includes some areas that had earlier been part of Bombay, Madhya Pradesh and Hyderabad states.
2. Land records are maintained under the Maharashtra Land Code 1966.[1] Its predecessor Acts are [Sec. 336]:
   (i) The Bombay City Land Revenue Act, 1876
   (ii) The Bombay Land Revenue Code 1879
   (iii) The Bombay City Survey Act, 1915
   (iv) The Central Provinces Land Alienation Act, 1916
   (v) The Bombay Revenue Tribunal Act, 1957
   (vi) The Madhya Pradesh Land Revenue Code 1954
   (vii) The Hyderabad Land Revenue Act, 1317-F
   (viii) The Hyderabad Record-of-Rights in Land Regulations 1358-F

Coverage of Urban Area

3. This code has detailed provisions for survey, preparation and updating of record-of-rights and other such matters for urban as well as rural areas. Most of the provisions are equally applicable to villages and cities, with certain special provisions

APPENDIX A: ANALYSIS OF LAWS ON RECORD-OF-RIGHTS IN SELECT STATES   141

for cities wherever required. Some important provisions in this regard are quoted here:

4. The dentition of village includes a town and city [Sec. 2(43)].
5. As per definition of *Gaothan* or 'village site', it means land included within the site of a village, town or city [Sec. 2(10)].
6. All land including non-agriculture land is liable to land revenue [Sec. 64].
7. Many provisions of the present land code are not applicable to the city of Bombay (Mumbai) [Sec. 1(2)].
8. There are special provisions in Chapter XIV about maintenance of records, assessment of land revenue and survey for the city of Bombay which are more or less similar to that for other areas of the state except that all the powers for maintenance of records, survey, correction of maps, etc., have been vested in the Collector.
9. Land in urban areas, whether used for agriculture or non-agricultural purposes, is also assessed for land revenue. While land used for residential purposes in a village is exempted from land revenue, land in cities used as such is not exempted automatically [Sec. 123].

Contents

10. Record-of-rights of every village and town includes the following particulars [Sec. 148]:

    (a) Names of all persons who are holders, occupants, owners or mortgagees of the land.
    (b) Names of all persons who are holding land as government lessees or tenants.
    (c) Nature and extent of the respective interests of such persons and the conditions or liabilities attached with such interest.
    (d) Rent or revenue payable by or to any such person.
    (e) Such order particulars as the State Government may prescribe by rules.

11. In Maharashtra, all persons holding land are classified as Occupants-Class I, Occupants-Class II, and Government

lessees. Occupants-Class I hold the land in perpetuity with full rights to transfer the land which actually amounts to ownership. Occupants-Class II also hold the land in perpetuity but have certain restrictions on transfer of land [Sec. 29].

12. A record of customs, called Wajib-ul-arz, in respect of right to irrigation, right of way, right of fishing or any other easement in land or water controlled by the government or local authority is also required to be made [Sec. 165].

Legal Sanctity

13. Any entry in the record-of-rights and a certified entry in the register of mutation shall be presumed to be true until the contrary is proved or a new entry is lawfully substituted therefor [Sec. 157].

14. The information in the booklet containing a copy of record-of-rights issued to the landowner under Sec. 151(3) will also be presumed to be true until the contrary is proved [Sec. 151(7)].

Administrative Machinery

15. A commissioner is appointed in each division with the requisite number of additional commissioners and assistant commissioners to assist him. A Collector is appointed in each district with required number of Additional Collectors and Deputy Collectors to assist him. A *tehsildar* and one or more *naib-tehsildars* are appointed in each subdivision of the district called *taluka*. An adequate number of circle officers, circle inspectors and *talathis* are appointed by the Collector to look after the work at the village level. The State Government may also appoint a settlement commissioner, director of land records and settlement officers as may appear necessary [Secs. 5-9].

Preparation of Records, Cadastral Survey, Involvement of the Community

16. The government, whenever it may seem expedient, can order a survey of any village, city or town for the purpose of making records and assessment of land revenue [Secs. 79, 83].

APPENDIX A: ANALYSIS OF LAWS ON RECORD-OF-RIGHTS IN SELECT STATES   143

17. When a record-of-rights is to be prepared for the first time in an area, the *talathi* issues a notice to the residents calling upon them to furnish information about their rights in the land within thirty days. On the basis of information so received and by local enquiry, a rough copy of record-of-rights is prepared and published for inviting objections. The objections are decided after hearing all the affected parties and the record is finalized in the presence of residents of that area and a fair copy is prepared. The fair copy of record is again published for inviting objections. The objections are decided by an officer not below the rank of a deputy collector in the presence of residents before finally publishing the record-of-rights for that area. An almost similar procedure is followed when a new record-of-rights is prepared to revise an existing record [Rules 4, 5, 6][2].

18. A person holding the land may be required to produce his title deeds at the time of original survey only. If the name of a person appears in the records, he will not be compelled to produce his title deeds in any subsequent survey. This means that an entry in the records will be taken as evidence of his title without any need for him to prove it during any subsequent survey [Sec. 88].

19. In towns and cities, the preparation of the record-of-right can also be ordered under Sec. 126 and in such cases the record is prepared as per provisions of the Maharashtra Land Revenue (Village, Town and City Survey) Rules, 1969. The ownership and possession is decided on the basis of the field inquiry and claims of the residents after hearing all the affected parties. This record will contain a cadastral map and property card in Form 'D'.[3]

20. After completion of the survey and preparation of property cards, the Collector will issue a '*sanad*' (equivalent to a title deed issued by the government) to all the occupiers of a building site in the Form given in Schedule C. This *sanad* confirms that this land will be with him in perpetuity with

full right to transfer. This *sanad*, in effect, is a certificate of title in favour of the landholder [Sec. 129].

21. After the survey in any area, boundaries of all survey numbers will be fixed and demarcated by boundary marks [Sec. 132].
22. On the application of any party, the boundary of a field is demarcated by government officials and any dispute regarding them is resolved after hearing all the parties [Secs. 135, 136].
23. There is a detailed procedure and obligation of land holders and survey officers to maintain boundary marks of survey numbers in good condition. In case of town planning which may require formation of plots, etc., the collector will cause to erect new boundary marks [Secs. 139-146].

Public Access to Records

24. All the maps and other records are open to public inspection and certified copies can be obtained by the people.

Regular Updating of Records

25. Every person is required, within three months, to give information of acquisition of a right in the land to the *talathi*, who gives a written receipt for the same. Persons acquiring a right with the permission of the collector or through a registered document are exempted from this provision. Information about such acquisition is required to be sent directly by the sub-registrar and collector to the *talathi*. In the cities, this information is to be sent to the Collector. The Collector may impose a penalty for not giving such information within the prescribed time [Secs. 149, 154]. In the case of registered deeds, the registrar has to send this information.
26. In the city of Mumbai, such information is to be given within 20 days to the Collector who gets necessary changes in the record-of-rights made on the basis of this information [Secs. 296, 297].
27. There is a very elaborate procedure for making any changes in the record-of-rights. First the *talathi* enters a mutation and posts a copy of the proposed changes at a conspicuous place in the

village. As soon as a mutation relating to a land is entered, the *talathi* makes a remark in the record-of-rights against the entry of that land, giving reference of the mutation register so that on inspection of the record-of-rights it is known that the land is the subject matter of a pending mutation. Then he sends written information to all the interested parties. On receipt of any objection, he enters it in a register and issues a written acknowledgement to the person making such an objection. All the disputed cases are decided by a superior revenue officer, following the laid-down procedure. No such case can be decided without giving notice to the affected party. After a final decision on mutation, the entry is transferred to the records-of-rights [Sec. 150].

Adjudication Procedures

28. Revenue officers, i.e., Commissioner, Collector, *Tehsildars*, etc., have the power to summon people and ask them to give evidence and produce documents. In case of failure to appear, the revenue officer may even issue a warrant of arrest [Secs. 227-229].
29. An inquiry under the Maharashtra Land Revenue Code is deemed to be a judicial proceeding within the meaning of Secs. 193, 219 and 228 of the IPC (relating to punishment for false evidence, illegal orders and contempt of courts) and the authority holding such an inquiry is deemed to be a civil court [Sec. 237].
30. The parties can engage legal professionals to represent their cases during the course of any inquiry [Sec. 244].
31. Appeals against the orders of subordinate officers lie before superior officers. A maximum of two appeals are permitted. There are provisions for review and revision of orders passed by a revenue officer [Secs. 247-249].

Role of Civil Courts

32. The jurisdiction of civil courts is excluded from actions taken under Secs. 36, 36A and 36B under which the land of a tribal

cannot be transferred to a non-tribal without the permission of the Collector [Sec. 36C].
33. A civil court cannot pass a decree or order in the case of a land, the occupancy of which is not transferable without the previous sanction of the Collector [Sec. 61].

Record-of-Rights in Karnataka

Preliminary

1. Karnataka (earlier Mysore) was formed by unifying the areas that comprised the erstwhile states/provinces of Coorg, Hyderabad, Madras and Bombay. Different revenue laws were applicable in different areas which had minor differences. The Karnataka Land Revenue Act, 1964[4] was enacted to unify all the laws.
2. This Act more or less follows the Maharashtra Land Revenue Code 1964.

Coverage of Urban Area

3. Sec. 2 (38): village includes cities and towns.
4. Sec. 80: all land, agriculture or non agriculture, are liable to land revenue. This means that this Act applies to land in urban areas also. Sec. 60 mentions this clearly in the definition of land.
5. Under Chapter IX, Sec. 106, the State Government can conduct a survey of any area including an urban area.

Contents

6. Provisions for ROR are contained in Chapter XI. Record-of-rights has to be prepared for every village. As per definition of village in Sec. 2 (38), it includes city and town also.
7. The provisions are similar to MLRC. Map and mutation registers are not mentioned in the list of record-of-rights..

Legal Sanctity

8. Sec. 133 gives the presumption of truth to entries in the record-of-rights, Mutation register and Patta book.

Administrative Machinery

9. Sec. 17: Village accountant to maintain land records/registers as prescribed.
Sec. 18: Survey officers responsible for survey, assessment and settlement.

10. Karnataka has provision to appoint licensed surveyors as per Sec. 18A. This is a progressive step which should be replicated in other states also.

Preparation of Records, Cadastral Survey, Involvement of the Community

11. Sec. 137 provides for procedure to fix boundaries of all survey numbers and resolving disputes on boundaries. Under Sec. 140, the *tehsildar* will decide boundary disputes. Sec. 141 provides for arbitration by arbitrators nominated by the parties.
12. It is obligatory on land owners to maintain boundary marks. There is a penalty for damaging them.
13. Chapter XIII provides for the survey of village sites and town and cities. Under Sec. 152, the State Government can order a survey of such lands as per provision of Secs. 106 and 112.

Public Access to Record-of-Rights

14. All the maps and land records are open to the public for inspection and applying for copies [Sec. 193].
15. Sec. 154 allows a person to seek a certificate from the *tehsildar* regarding his holding.

Regular Updating of Records

16. There is a specific provision for division of survey numbers (Sec. 109) whenever required.
17. Sec. 128: It is the duty of a person to report any acquisition of right within three months to the village officer who will give a written acknowledgement to him. A person acquiring a right by registered deed is exempted from the provision of sending information, because in such cases information is sent by the sub-registrar directly.
18. In case a right is acquired through partition, a map made by a licensed surveyor has to be attached. This is a good provision to reduce the work of revenue officials and provide quick service to the people. Sec. 109(2) provides for appointment of

senior officers for receiving such reports who will forward it to the village officer. This reform is required in every state. The report should be received by a senior officer having a stationary and continuously functioning office. It is difficult to locate the village officer because of the nature of his duties. There is a penalty for not reporting acquisition of rights.

19. Entry of reports in the mutation register and sanction are similar to MLRC. All disputed cases are decided by a senior officer. Before transferring these entries from the mutation register to the record-of-rights, the entries are to be confirmed by a prescribed officer.

20. Sec.129-A makes it mandatory to issue a *patta* book to each landowner and update it time to time as per rules. In Maharashtra, it is optional for the landowner to demand a booklet. However in Karnataka it is mandatory.

21. Every person has the obligation to provide any record or document needed to correct records as and when demanded by a revenue officer. There is a penalty for non-compliance.

22. Sec 131 (c) is a unique provision where it is mandatory for any person who is dividing his plot for sale or otherwise to get a sketch prepared by a licensed surveyor. This sketch is required to be attached with a report regarding acquisition of right to the revenue officer. Such a sketch is also to be presented to the sub-registrar for registration of the deed. Thus, in Karnataka, along with the sale deed, a map of the land has to be attached.

23. Sec. 132 provides for a mechanism to keep records updated. Any civil court or any other court will not accept an application or suit relating to land unless a copy of the record-of-rights or mutation register is attached. After the decision, the court will convey the required correction to the Deputy Commissioner who will get the records corrected as per the decree. This decree is supposed to be registered with the sub registrar-also as per the Registration Act.

Adjudication Procedures

24. Chapter III specifies the procedure of revenue officers. Every officer exercising powers under this Act is a revenue court. In Maharashtra and Punjab, the term 'Revenue Court' has not been used so clearly. A Revenue Court (Sec. 28) has the power to take evidence on oath and summon persons to give evidence, produce documents, etc. All persons so summoned are bound to comply. The revenue officer may issue a warrant also as under the MLRC (Sec. 32).
25. There is a Land Appellate Tribunal at the state level comprising six members out of which three are serving district judges and others are officers having experience in land administration. Proceedings before the tribunal are judicial proceedings. Sec. 45 says the orders of the Tribunal will be final and will not be called in question in any court.
26. An elaborate and well- defined procedure for appeal and review of orders passed by any revenue officer is there in Chapter V. Only two appeals are allowed.
27. Provisions regarding appeal and revision do not apply to sanction of mutation. Only one appeal is allowed against an order of confirmation of entry. An order in this appeal is final. This provision is there to quickly finalize the record-of-rights.

Role of Civil Courts

28. The jurisdiction of civil courts is barred in matters relating to this Act. Sec. 61. Sec. 62 provides certain exceptions to this provision. Basically, the jurisdiction of civil courts is barred from interfering in the proceedings under the Act and for any claim against the government. However, people are allowed to go to civil courts to establish their private rights. A plaintiff is supposed to exhaust his right to appeal before going to the civil courts.
29. Sec. 64 and Sec. 65 provide for referring a question to a High Court by the Tribunal and to a civil court when there is grey area whether the case falls under the jurisdiction of a civil or a

revenue court. This provision is to save landowners from unnecessary litigation due to conflicting opinions of civil courts and revenue courts. In Punjab, this provision is not there.

30. Sec. 135 gives an option to people to seek remedy under the Specific Relief Act, 1877 for declaration of right. Records will be corrected as per orders of the court.

Record-of-Rights in Punjab

Preliminary

1. The Punjab Land Revenue Act was enacted in 1887.[5] It has been amended many times afterwards but the basic scheme has not changed. Its predecessor Act was the Punjab Land Revenue Act, 1871.
2. Described as 'An Act to amend and declare the law in force in Punjab with respect to making and maintenance of records of rights in land....'
3. Definition of landowner includes any person who is getting a profit from the land.
4. Estate is a village, unit of assessment of Land Revenue.

Coverage of Urban Area

5. Sec. 4 excludes 'site of a village' which is not assessed to land revenue from operation of this Act. However, an explanation clarifies that all the land within a municipal area will be covered. So this Act is applicable on land in the cities.

Contents

6. Sec. 31 provides for making record-of-rights which will include
   (a) A statement containing:
      (i) Names of the landowners, tenants and other persons entitled to receive any share from the profit or produce of the land.
      (ii) Nature and extent of interest and conditions and liabilities attached thereto.
      (iii) Rent, revenue, rates, cess due from each person.
   (b) A statement of customs respecting rights and liabilities in the estate.
   (c) A map of the estate.
7. Every year a new edition of register of land owners (*jamabandi*) is made after incorporating changes made during the previous year. In practice, a new edition is prepared after every five

years. Maps and statement of customs are not revised every five years. These are reviewed at the time of settlement only when record is prepared afresh. No changes are incorporated in maps because these are on paper and repeated handling may damage them. Also, these are kept in the custody of the Collector to avoid any tampering. However, the division of a land parcel is shown in the copies of the map kept with the Assistant Collector and village *Patwari*.

8. Register of ownership is indexed as per landowners. However, there is another register called *Khasra Girdawari*, which is indexed on the plot number.

Legal Sanctity

9. Sec. 44 of the Act gives presumptive status to the entries of the record-of-rights unless proved otherwise. Any entry in the record-of-rights or annual records shall be presumed true until the contrary is proved or the entry is substituted as per procedure and law.
10. Sec. 151(2): A village officer with respect to records and papers kept by him is deemed to be a public officer within the meaning of the Indian Evidence Act, 1872, having custody of public documents which any person has the right to inspect.

Administrative Machinery

11. A range of revenue officers are appointed under Sec. 6 to dispose of the work under the Act—Financial Commissioner, Commissioner, Collector, Assistant Collector Grade I and AC Grade II.
12. Provision for appointment of other officers, i.e., *Kannongo*, *Patwaris*, village officers (*Lambardars*).
    Preparation of Records, Cadastral Survey, Involvement of the Community
13. There are detailed provisions in the Act for survey and fixation of boundaries. The entire chapter VIII is devoted to this subject. Sec. 100 empowers the Financial Commissioner to make rules

in respect of demarcation of boundaries and erection of survey marks. However, no such rules have been made. The land settlement manual written 100 years ago is a guide book without any legal force.

14. Sec. 101 empowers a revenue officer to define the boundaries of any parcel of land and erect survey marks.
15. Sec. 107 enables the government to appoint any other agency for survey of lands.
16. As per the old procedure, copies of land records are given only to landowners or interested parties and not to any third party. However, with the RTI Act in place, any one can obtain copies of records of anyone else.
17. Sec. 37 (c) says no change of entry without making new maps where it is necessary. So, the Act mandates making a new map on division of the land parcel before making changes in ownership records. However, this provision is not implemented properly.

Regular Updating of Records

18. Sec. 34 makes it mandatory on any one acquiring a right in land to report it to the *Patwari*. He enters every such report in the register of mutation. There is a fine under Sec. 39 for not reporting within three months but it can be imposed by the Collector at his discretion which is almost never imposed. There should be a consequence of not reporting like in the Registration Act where non-registration results in a document not presentable as evidence. A receipt regarding reporting can be made mandatory whenever a registered document is produced as evidence. Also, a person should be allowed to send this information by post or e-mail to the Assistant Collector also who may in turn send it to the *Patwari* or may enter the mutation himself where records are computerized.
19. He can enter a mutation *suo moto* also on the basis of his information without any application.
20. All such mutations will be examined by the assistant collector and will be sanctioned if found correct.

APPENDIX A: ANALYSIS OF LAWS ON RECORD-OF-RIGHTS IN SELECT STATES

21. The Act provides for a procedure but no time limit for informing acquisition of such right or a time limit for inquiry by a revenue officer is mentioned. There is no format for application and time stamped receipts. This leads to non-updating of records and uncertainty about the up-to-date status of records. Whenever a mutation is entered, a remark is made in the account of the landowner so the fact about the existence of a claim is known to every interested person even if mutation is not sanctioned. Sec. 35 gives the power to the *Patwari* to record undisputed acquisition of interest as per the prescribed rule. Perhaps, there are no rules in this regard and it leads to the discretion of the *Patwari* to make changes in the records.

Adjudication Procedures

22. Sec. 36(1) gives the power to the revenue officer to make an inquiry as he deems fit and decide the matter in case of any dispute regarding what entry is to be made. This dispute may arise during the course of any inquiry, making of any record. This action can be taken on the application of a person or *suo moto* by the revenue officer.
23. Sec. 36(20) gives the power to decide on possession and hand over possession to the person best entitled to such possession, subject to the passing of any further order by a court of competent jurisdiction.
24. Sec. 37 however provides that no entry will be changed without the facts proved or admitted. This restricts powers under Sec. 36 to some extent but needs more clarity in the drafting. There are many court decisions on this issue. The opinion of the courts should be incorporated in the Act.
25. Chapter IX is devoted to partition of land. The revenue officer is empowered to partition land on an application of a co-sharer. If there is any question as to title, he may advise the parties to get it settled in a civil court or he may himself proceed to act as a civil court and pass a decree. This order will be appealable in the court of the district judge. This is a unique provision where

the revenue officer temporarily assumes the powers of a civil court. However, he is not trained for this work and this provision only prolongs litigation. It advisable that the question of title is decided in the civil courts only.

26. Sec. 121 empowers a revenue officer to give possession to any party as per an order in the partition proceedings. This is a unique power because generally dispossession can be done only on the basis of a decree of the civil court.
27. Sec. 123 provides for affirmation by a revenue officer of the partition made by the parties themselves.
28. Chapter X provides for appointment of arbitrators for resolving any dispute regarding boundaries, revenue entry, partition, etc. The award of the arbitrators is to be accepted by the revenue officer. Further appeal will lie before a superior revenue officer.
29. Under Sec. 136, to facilitate the making of the record-of-rights in an area, a revenue officer can be given powers of the civil court to decide disputes arising in the course of making records.
30. Sec. 141: Revenue officer will execute the decrees issued in respect of land and any interest in land.
31. Sec. 149: Provision of fine for not attending proceedings before a revenue officer.
32. Sec. 13 provides for appeal. Any order of a revenue officer, whether original or as an appellate authority, can be appealed before the next superior officer. However, no second appeal is acceptable if the original order is confirmed by the appellate authority. In case the order is modified or reversed in appeal by the Collector, the order of the Commissioner in further appeal will be final. This means that an appeal against the original order of the Assistant Collector will not go beyond the Commissioner.
33. Sec. 15 provides for review of his own orders by a revenue officer on the application of any interested party. However, the permission of a superior authority is required in certain cases. The order will not be modified on review without giving an opportunity to all the affected parties.

34. Sec. 16 provides for revision of any order of subordinate revenue officers by the Financial Commissioner but not without giving an opportunity to the affected parties.
35. The revenue officer is empowered to summon any person in the course of any proceedings before him. As per the Act, such a person is bound to state the truth before a revenue officer.
36. A legal practitioner can appear on behalf a person in any proceedings.

Role of Civil Courts

37. Sec. 45 gives an opportunity to persons to institute a suit for declaration under the Specific Relief Act, 1877. The Act should clarify the points on which appeals will be heard by the revenue officer and the points on which a person should seek a decree of the court. This principle can be decided on the basis of various court rulings.
38. Sec. 158: Exclusion of jurisdiction of civil courts. No civil court will have jurisdiction over matters which a revenue officer is authorized to dispose of exercising the powers under the Act.

Miscellaneous

39. Sec. 46 gives rule-making powers to the Financial Commissioner for prescribing forms, language, procedures for survey, conduct of inquiries, etc. However, such rules have never been made. Generally, procedures are guided by three manuals compiled about 100 years ago and which are not legally enforceable.
40. Sec. 48 exempts all land up to 5 acres from payment of land revenue. So fiscal purpose of land records is hardly relevant.
41. As per practice, land belonging to a Hindu undivided family is recorded in the name of the head of the family. However, the land belongs to all the coparceners. The legal backing of this provision gives rise to disputes where the father can sell land without the consent of other members of the family. This issue may also give rise to some disputes. Explanation I of Sec.

48 says that for assessment purposes, the land of an HUF will be assumed to be land of the head of the family with a limit of five acres.
42. Sec.48-A provides for land revenue on non-agricultural land also.
43. Sec. 61 makes all the landowners jointly and severally responsible for payment of total land revenue for that estate.
44. Rules are required to be made under the following provisions:
   (i) Sec. 17(1): Procedure before a revenue officer; rule made by notification dated 1.03.1888
   (ii) Sec. 35 (a) regarding recording of undisputed entries by the *Patwari*.
   (iii) Sec. 46 regarding making of record-of-rights.
   (iv) Sec. 100: Demarcation of boundaries and erection of survey marks.
   (v) Sec. 155: Rules to give effect to various provisions of this Act.

Record-of-Rights in West Bengal

Preliminary

1. The land records are maintained under the provisions of the West Bengal Land Reforms Act, 1955.[6] This Act was enacted by repealing a number of previous Acts like the Bengal Tenancy Act, 1885, The Cooch Behar Tenancy Act, 1910, the Bengal Rent Act, 1859, etc.
2. All the persons actually holding the land, called *raiyat*, have become owners with full rights to transfer and inheritance [Sec. 4].

Coverage of Urban Area

3. This Act extends to all the rural and urban area of the State except a part of area included in Kolkata Municipal Corporation. The State Government has authority to include this left-out area also by issuing a notification [Sec. 1(2)].

Contents

4. The State Government can order preparation or revision of record-of-rights any time in any area of the State [Sec. 51].
5. A large-scale map for each village (which includes a city also) showing all the fields, homesteads and other physical features like roads, rivers, railways, etc., is prepared by cadastral survey. Each plot in the village is assigned a unique five-digit identification number.[7]
6. A separate statement of rights called *'Khatian'* is prepared for each land holder which contains the following particulars:[8]
    (i) Name of person holding the land (*raityat*), name of the landlord and conditions of tenancy.
    (ii) Area, location and classification of land.
    (iii) Rights and obligations of *raityat* in respect of use, repair and maintenance of appliances for irrigation.
    (iv) Details of right of way or other easement.

7. Land revenue and cess payable to facilitate search of status of a particular plot, a plot number.

Legal Sanctity

8. An entry in the record-of-rights is presumed to be correct subject to any order in appeal as per provisions of the Act [Sec. 51A (9)].

Administrative Machinery

9. For the preparation, maintenance, adjudication and other matters related to record-of-rights at the State level, there is a Board of Revenue and a Director of Land Records and Surveys.
10. Further below, there are five tiers of land and land reforms administration, namely, division, district, sub-division, block and gram panchayat which function under the Commissioner, Collector, Sub-divisional Land & land Reforms Officer, Block Land & Land Reforms officer and Revenue Inspector.

Preparation of Records, Cadastral Survey, Involvement of the Community

11. At the time of preparation or revision of record-of-rights, land holders are involved at various stages as prescribed in the rules. Finally, a draft record-of-rights is published for inviting objections. Objections can be filed up to one year before an officer empowered for this purpose. Further appeal against an order of such an officer is also allowed. No correction in any entry can be made without hearing all the concerned parties [Sec. 51A].
12. The scale of cadastral mapping is 16" to 1 mile in rural areas and 32" to 1 mile in semi-urban area. In urban areas, maps are prepared on the scale of 64" to 1 mile, 128" to I mile or 1" to 50 feet. The present survey, started in 1972, is nearing completion. Earlier surveys were conducted during 1888-1940 and 1954-1962.[9]

13. The boundaries between plots are accurately fixed and shown to land holders before final publication of records.

Regular Updating of Records

14. The record-of-rights is regularly updated to incorporate changes due to transfer, inheritance, partition, new government grants and other similar reasons [Sec. 50].
15. The application for mutation can be filed in the office of the Revenue Inspector or in any higher office of the Land and Land Reforms Department. The Revenue Inspector makes a field inquiry and submits a report to the Block Land and Land Reforms Officer. An order on the mutation application is made on the basis of a field inquiry by the Revenue Inspector and hearing by the Revenue Officer.[10]
16. The record-of-rights is updated by the especially empowered Revenue Officer on the basis of a mutation order or any such other order. Parties are informed about the changes made in the records [Rule 21][11].

Adjudication Procedures

17. An appeal can be filed against the orders of the revenue officers to the superior officers. An order passed in appeal is final. However the State Government can pass any order to correct any order of any revenue officer [Sec. 54].
18. Officers dealing with proceedings under the Act will have the powers of a civil court to summon, ask for production of documents, etc. [Sec. 57].

Role of Civil Courts

19. During the process of preparation or revision of record-of-rights, civil courts are barred from entertaining any suit in related matters. Further, no civil court will entertain any suit or application regarding correction of an entry in the record-of-rights [Sec. 51C].
20. The civil courts have no jurisdiction to determine any question relating to any matter which is to be decided by a revenue

officer under the Act. However, this bar on jurisdiction will not affect any right which the parties to any dispute may have against each other [Sec. 61].

NOTES

1. (The Maharashtra Land Revenue Code 1966)
2. (Maharashtra Land Revenue Record-of-Rights and Registers (Preparation and Maintenance) Rule 1971)
3. (Maharashtara Land Revenue (Village, Town and City survey) Rules 1969)
4. (The Karnataka Land Revenue Act, 1964)
5. (The Punjab Land Revenue Act, 1887)
6. (The West Bengal Land Reforms Act, 1955)
7. (The West Bengal Land Reforms Rules 1965), Schedule A
8. (The West Bengal Land Reforms Rules 1965), Rule 23
9. (website, Land and Land Reforms Department, Government of West Begal)
10. (The West Bengal Land and Land Reforms Manual 1991)
11. (The West Bengal Land Reforms Rules 1965)

Bibliography

Annual Report, Ministry of Rural Development. Government of India, 2006-07.

Barnett, Walter E. "Marketable Title Acts: Panacea or Pandemonium." *Cornell Law Review* 53, no. 1 (1967): 45-97.

Carruthers, Penny. "A Tangled Web Indeed: The English Land Registration Act and Comparison with the Australian Torrens System." *UNSW Law Journal* (UNSW Law School) 18, no. 4 (2015): 1261-1299.

"Decree No. 55-22 of 4 January 1955 on the reform of registration of land." The Government of French Republic, 1955.

"European Discovery and the Colonisation of Australia." *Australian Government*. June 4, 2017. http://www.australia.gov.au/about-australia/australian-story/european-discovery-and-colonisation (accessed June 4, 2017).

"Explanatory Notes, Land Registration Act." The National Archives on behalf of HM Government of UK, 2002.

"French Civil Code." Government of French Republic.

Gardner, Simon. "The Land Registration Act, 2002—the Show on the Road." *The Modern Law Review*, 2014: 763-779.

"General Law Land." *Victoria State Government*. https://www.propertyandlandtitles.vic.gov.au/__data/assets/pdf_file/0024/53817/General-Law-Land.pdf (accessed June 8, 2017).

"German Civil Code." Federal Republic of Germany.

Gil, Stéphane. "The French Land Administration." Permanent Committee on Cadastre in the European Union, 2002.

Glok, stephane. *Real Property Law and Procedure in the EU—National Report France*. European University Institute, 2016.

Great Britain. *Acquisition and Valuation of Land Committee, Fourth report*. London: His Majesty's Stationery Office, 1919.

Hawerk, Winfried. *Grandbuch and Cadastral Systems in Germany, Austria and Switzerland*. paper in conference, Commission 7, Cadastre and Rural Land Management, International Federation of Surveyors (FIG), 1995.

Hendrik Ploeger, Aart van Velten and Jaap Zevenbergen. "Real Property Law and Procedure in the EU-Report for the Netherlands." European University Institute, 2016.

Hogg, James Edward. "Registration of Title to Land." *The Yale Law Journal* (The Yale Law Journal Company) 28, no. 1 (1918): 51-58.

Hogg, James Edward. *Registration of Title to Land Throughout the Empire*. Sweet & Maxwell Limited, London, 1920.

Iyer, Abhijit Banerjee and Lakshmi. "History, Institutions, and Economic Performance: The Legacy of Colonial Land Tenure Systems in India." (American Economic Association) September 2005.

Justin T Holl, Peter Rabley, Mark Monacelli, David Ewan. "The Earthen Vessel: Land Records in the United States." *PRIYA Annual Winter Conference*, Washington, DC, 2010.

Kadaster, Netherlands. "Land Transaction and Registration Process in the Netherlands." IPRA-CINDER, International Centre for Registration Law.

Krishna Iyer, V. R. "Intricacies of Property Law, Book Review of 'Transfer of Property Act, 1882' by M. R. Mallick." *The Hindu*, October 23, 2001.

"Land and Property Information, New South Wales Government." http://www.lpi.nsw.gov.au/land_titles/land_ownership/old_system (accessed June 4, 2017).

"Land Registration Act." Government of the United Kingdom, 2002.

"Land Registry Act, 1962." Government of the United Kingdom.

"Land Registry Act, Grandbuchordnung-GBO." Federal Ministry of Justice and Consumer Protection, Germany.

"Land Titles." *Victoria State Government*. http://www.dtpli.vic.gov.au/property-and-land-titles/land-titles/about-land-titles/general-law-land (accessed June 7, 2017).

Land Titling - A Road Map. Department of Land Resources, Government of India, 2014.

"Land Transfer Act, 1875." Government of the United Kingdom.

Law Commission of India. "157th Report on the Transfer of Property Act." Law Commission, 1998.

Law Commission of India. "Seventieth Report on the Transfer of Property Act." 1977.

Law Commission of India. "Sixth Report on the Registration Act." 1957.

Law Reforms Commission Ontario. *Report on Land Registration.* Department of Justice, Ontario, Canada, 1971.

Louwman, Wim. "Advantages and Disadvantages of a Merger Organisation: The Case of the Kadaster—Netherlands." 2017.

Louwman, Wim. "The Integration of the Cadastre and Public Registers in the Netherlands." Permanent Committee on Cadastre in the European Union.

"Maharashtra Land Revenue (Village, Town and City Survey) Rules." Government of Maharashtra, 1969.

"Maharashtra Land Revenue Record of Rights and Registers (Preparation and Maintenance) Rule." Government of Maharashtra, 1971.

McCormack, John L. "Torrens and Recording: Land Title Assurance in the Computer Age." *William Mitchell Law Review* (Mitchell Hamline School of Law) 18, no. 1 (1992): 61-129.

Mulla, Sir Dinshaw Fardunji. *The Registration Act.* 13th edition. LexisNexis, 2016.

National Commission to Review the Working of the Constitution. Ministry of Law, Justice and Company Affairs, Government of India, 2002.

Nettle, Kevin. "Title vs Deeds: International Experience and Implication for India." *World Bank Workshop on 'Land Policies for Accelerated Growth and Poverty Reduction in India".* 2006.

Norman, Paul E. *Photogrammetry and the Cadastral Survey.* ITC, 1965.

O'Connor, Pamela. "Deferred and Immediate Indefeasibility: Bijural

Ambiguity in Registered Land Title Systems." *Faculty of Law, Monash University*, 2009: 193-223.

O'Connor, Pamela. "Double Indemnity—Title Insurance and Torrens System." *Queensland University of Technology Law and Justice Journal* 3, no. 1 (2003).

O'Connor, Pamela. "The Top 10 Legal Questions for Registered Title Systems." In *Property and Security: Selected Essays*, by Brendan Edgeworth, Cathy Sherry Lyria Bennett Moses. Thomson Reuters Australia, 2010.

PRS Legislative Research. *http://www.prsindia.org/theprsblog/?p=1033.* (accessed February 22, 2018).

Ramanathan, Swati. "Security of Title to Land in Urban Areas." *India Infrastructure Report* (Oxford University Press), 2009: 20-28.

"Real Property Act (SA)." Government of South Australia, Australia, 1886.

Real Property Law and Procedure in the European Union. National Report Germany, European University Institute, Florence, 2005.

Ruoff, Theodore B. F. "An Englishman Looks at the Torrens System." *Australian Law Journal*, 1952.

Scottish Law Commission. "Discussion Paper on Land Registration: Void and Voidable Titles." February 2004.

Simpson, S. Rowton. *Land Law and Registration.* London: Surveyor's Publications (part of the Royal Institution of Chartered Surveyors), 1976.

Sinha, Rita. "Moving Towards Clear Land titles In India." *Innovation in Land Rights Recognition, Administration, and Governance.* The World Bank, 2010.

Sparkes, Peter. *Real Property Law and Procedure in the EU—Report from England and Wales.* European University Institute, 2016.

Standing Committee on Rural Development, Sixteenth Lok Sabha. *Ninth Report of Standing Committee on the Registration (Amendment) Bill 2013.* Lok Sabha Secretariat, 2015.

Stein, R. "The 'Principles, Aims, and Hopes' of Title by Registration." *Adelaide Law Review* (Adelaide Law Review Association, School of Law, University of Adelaide) 9, no. 2 (1983): 267-278.

"The Karnataka Land Revenue Act." Government of Karnataka, 1964.

The Land Registry, The Government of Hong Kong Special Administrative Region. http://www.landreg.gov.hk/en/title/ordinance.htm (accessed June 15, 2017).

"The Maharashtra Land Revenue Code." Government of Maharashtra, 1966.

The McKinsey Global Institute. "India: The Growth Imperative." 2001.

"The National Land Records Modernization Programme, Guidelines, Technical Manuals and MIS." Government of India, 2008-09.

"The Punjab Land Revenue Act." Government of Punjab, 1887.

"The Registration Act." Government of India, 1908.

"The Transfer of Property Act." Government of India, 1882.

"The West Bengal Land and Land Reforms Manual." Board of Revenue, Government of West Bengal, 1991.

"The West Bengal Land Reforms Act." Government of West Bengal, 1955.

"The West Bengal Land Reforms Rules." Government of West Bengal, 1965.

Torrens, Robert R. *The South Australian System of Conveyancing by Registration of Title.* Adelaide, 1859.

Town and Country Planning Organisation, Government of India." Model Guidelines For Urban Land Policy(draft)." July 2007.

Uniform Law Commission, the United States. "Model Marketable Title Act." Model Act, 1990.

"Updating the Land Registration Act, 2002: A Consultation Paper, Summary." Law Commission, England, March 2016.

Vliet, Lars van. "Transfer of Property Inter Vivos." *Maastricht European Private Law Institute*, 2017.

Wadhwa, D. C. "Guaranteeing Title to Land: A Preliminary Study." *Economic and Political Weekly*, October 1989: 2323-2334.

Wadhwa, D. C. "Guaranteeing Title to Land: The Only Sensible

Solution." *Economic and Political Weekly* 37, no. 47 (November 2002): 4699-4722.

Willem Jan Wakker, Paul van der Molen, Christian Lemmen. "Land Registration and Cadastre in the Netherlands, and the role of cadastral boundaries." *Journal of Geospatial Engineering* (The Hong Kong Institution of Engineering Surveyors) 5, no. 1 (June 2003): 3-10.

Wilsch, Harald. "The German "Grundbuchordnung": History, principles and future about land registry in Germany." *zfv, Journal of Geodsey, Geoinformation and Land Management*, 2012.

World Bank. *Indian Land Policies for Growth and Poverty Reduction.* World Bank, 2007.

Zasloff, Jonathan. "India's Land Title Crisis:The Unanswered Questions." *Law Review* XX, no. X (2011).

Zevenbergen, J.A. "Overselling the Mirror and Curtain Principles of Land Titling." *Responsible Land Governance: Towards Evidence Based Approach*. Washington, D.C.: World Bank, 2017.

Zevenbergen, Jaap. *System of Land Registration, Aspects and Effects.* Netherlands Geodetic Commission, 2002.

Index

Adjudication Process, 85
All Property Transactions not Registered, 77
Assurance Fund, 66
Australia, 11, 40-50, 56, 58, 66, 73, 86, 95, 107, 112
   Deed Registration, 42, 48
   First Registration, 111
   History of Land Ownership, 41
     Indefeasibility of Registered Title, 44
     Indefeasibility of the Title of Volunteers, 45
     Exceptions to Indefeasibility of Torrens Title, 45
     Indemnity by the State, 46
     Restrictions on Indemnity, 47
     Maps and Boundaries of Land, 48
     Private Conveyancing, 41
     Qualified and Limited Titles, 49
     Title Registration, 40, 42, 47
     Process, 43
Australian Torrens Acts, 71
Austria, 11, 15, 59

Belgium, 15
Bengal Regulation XXXVI of 1793, 77
Bombay Presidency by Regulation IV of 1802, 77
Boundary and Cadastre, 112
Brazil, 15, 116

Cadastre Organization Act, 34
Cadastre, 61, 64
Canada, 15
Captain Arthur Phillip, 41
Carruthers, Penny, 71
China, 15
Chinks in Curtain, 71
Colorado, 24
Common law, 89
Compulsory Registration of All Transactions, 126
Compulsory Registration of Wills, 130
Conclusiveness of registered title, 71
Cook County, 23
County Council, 52, 53
Crown Lands Act, 1861, 41
Curtain principle, 10, 67-68, 70, 73-74, 108
Czechoslovakia, 59

Dayabhaga, 114-15
Deed Registration System, 2, 6, 77
   Constitutive Effect of, 95
   Effect of, 7
   Not Conclusive Proof of Title, 7
Denmark, 15
Description of Houses and Land by Reference to Government Maps of Surveys, 123
Description of Property and Maps or Plans, 122
District Land Registrar, 54
Draft Land Title Bill 2011, 103

England and Wales, Present Status of Registration in, 58
England, 50-59, 66, 73, 86, 89, 95, 110, 112-13

Alteration and Rectification Register, 57
Conclusiveness of Registered Title, 55
Charges, Notices and Restrictions, 56
Earlier System of Conveyancing, 50
Experience of England with Title Registration, 58
Failure of Early Title Registration Legislations, 51
First Registration, 111
Indemnity by the State, 57
Over-riding Interests, 56
Process of Registration, 54
Reforms in English Property Law, 52
Registration of Title under Land Registration Act, 2002, 54
Review of Land Registration Act, 1925, 53
Title Registration, 50-51, 59
English Group, 60
English Law, Influence of, 89

Federal Notary Law, 65
Field Measurement Book, 83
Fiji, 11, 109
Finland, 15
France, 15, 31, 79, 116
   Cadastre, 31
     and Real Estate File in Conformity, 33
   Deed Registration in, 28, 32
   Determination of Property Boundaries, 33
   Effect of Registration, 28
   Process of Registration, 29
   Provisional Registration, 30
   Role of Notary, 29
   Standardized Formats for Conveyance Deeds, 30
   Real Estate File, 31
   Registry Liable for Incorrect Information, 30

Georgia, 24
German Civil Code, 85
German Federal Constitution, 66
German Group, 60
German Land Register, 63, 67
German, 65, 66, 105
Germany, 11, 15, 59-60, 62, 79, 86, 95, 107, 109, 112-13
   Cadastre, 63
   Correction of Land Register, 65
   Indemnity for Loss, 66
   Institutional Structure, 64
   Land Register, 63
     Numerus Clausus, 60
     German Civil Code, 61
     Procedure for Registration, 61
   Principle of Abstract Nature of Rights, 64
   Registration, Effect, 62
   Role of Notary, 65
   Title Registration, 59
     History, 60
     Indefeasibility of, 62
     Law and Procedure, 60
Grantor-grantee index, 20
Greece, 15

Hindu Succession Act, 114
HM Land Registry, 53
Hogg, James Edward, 12, 14
Hong Kong, 15, 109, 117
Hungary, 59

Indefeasible, 105
Indemnity, 108
   First Resort and Last Resort Models, 109
   Resources for Fund, 109
India, 1, 3-5, 7-9, 13-15, 60, 76-100, 103, 105, 113-118, 120, 126-28, 130, 135
   Relevance of Title Registration, 102
India Land Policies for Growth and Poverty Reduction, 86

INDEX 171

Indian Contract Act, 1872, 89
Indian Registration Act, 1908, 89
Indian Succession Act, 114
Indian System, Strengths, 94
Indonesia, 15
Insurance, 70
  Principle, 10, 67
Inventory, 63
Israel, 11
Italy, 15, 116
Iyer, Justice V.R. Krishna, 90

Japan, 15, 116
Justice, equity and good conscience, 88

Kanan, Justice K., 127
Karnataka, Record-of-Rights, 147
  Adjudication Procedures, 150
  Administrative Machinery, 147
  Coverage of Urban Area, 147
  Legal Sanctity, 147
  Preparation of Records, Cadastral Survey, Involvement of the Community, 148
  Public Access to Record-of-Rights, 148
  Regular Updating of Records, 148
  Role of Civil Courts, 150
Kevin Nettle, 76

Land Register, 31, 61, 64-65, 86
Land Registration Act, 1925, 53-54, 56
Land Registration Act, 2002, 55-57
Land Registry, 66
Land Registry Act, 1862, 104
Land Transfer Act, 1875, 52
Land Transfer Act, 1897, 52
Law Commission, 53, 58
Law Commission of India, 124
Law of Property Act, 52
Law on Transfer of Property, 88
Lord Brougham, 88
Luxembourg, 15

Madras Presidency by Regulation XVII of 1802, 77
Mahalwari system, 83
Maharashtra, Record-of-Rights in, 140
  Adjudication Procedures, 145
  Administrative Machinery, 142
  Legal Sanctity, 142
  Preparation of Records, Cadastral Survey, Involvement of the Community, 142
  Public Access to Records, 144
  Regular Updating of Records, 144
  Role of Civil Courts, 145
  Urban Area, 140
Maintenance of land records, 4
Malaysia, 11, 15, 109
Mayor of Lyons v. East India Company, 88
McCormack, John L., 72
Merger of Cadastre and Registration Offices, 113
  Registration of Hereditary Rights, 114
Mirror principle, 70-71, 105
Mirror Works Other Way Round, 70
Mirror, 10, 67
Mitakshara, 114-15
Mortgages, 93
  by Deposit of Deeds, 131
  Mortgage by Deposit of Deeds, 94

Napoleon I, 31
National Land Records Modernization Program (NLRMP), 3, 102-3, 113
Negative system, 13
New Zealand, 11
Non-Banking Financial Companies (NBFC), 93
Norman, 13
North Carolina, 24
Northern Ireland, 50
Notarial Procedural Law, 65
Numerus Clausus Principle, 105

Ohio, 24
Ontario Law Reform Commission, 14
Ottoman Group, 60
Over-riding interests, 110

Parcel-wise Record on Land Title, 81
Poland, 15, 59
Portugal, 15
Positive system, 13
Presumption of Correctness, 85
Presumption of truth, 96
Prompt Disposal of Disputes by Revenue Officers, 133
Prussian Land Register Code of 1872, 60
Public faith, 62
Public register, 34
Punjab, Record-of-Rights in, 152
    Adjudication Procedures, 155
    Administrative Machinery, 153
    Coverage of Urban Area, 152
    Legal Sanctity, 153
    Regular Updating of Records, 154
    Role of Civil Courts, 157

Qualified indefeasibility, 72

Raiyatwari system, 83
Ramanathan, Swati, 2, 99
Real Estate File, 116
Real Property, 52
Real Property Act, 1858, 40
Record of Pending Litigation, 128
Record-of-Rights, 80, 83
    Alteration, 132
    Entry in as Constructive Notice, 138
    Land Parcel-wise, 95
    Presumption of Truth to, 96
    Process of Preparing, 84
    Recording Objections, 136
    Reducing Gap between Acquisition of Right and Entry, 134
    Updating, 84
Rectification of the Title Register, 112
Registered Title

Balance between Static, 108
Dynamic Security of Title, 108
Deferred Indefeasibility, 107
Dynamic Security of Title, 106
Indefeasibility of, 105
Protection to Volunteers, 107
Static Security of Title, 106
Registrar, Indexes Maintained, 79
Registration (Amendment) Bill 2013, 130-31
Registration Act, 1908, 5, 76
Registration
    Systems, 14
    Gap, 132
    Effect of, 78
    Procedure for, 78
    Proof of Ownership Time, 120
    Reducing Gap between Execution and, 131
Registration of
    Deeds Act, 1925, 42
    Title, 10, 95
Registration with Reference to Particular Property, 12
Registry, Search of Records of, 96
    Encumbrance Certificate, 97
Reserve Bank of India, 96
Right in Property, 126
Risk assumption, 27
Risk elimination, 27
Root of title, 8
Royal Commission, 51-52, 58

Scotland, 50
Scotland, Deed Registration, 13
Setalvad, M.C., 127
Shariat laws, 114
Sinha, Smt. Rita, 99
South Australia, 54
Spain, 15
State Indemnity, Limitations of, 73
State of Victoria, 49
Succession, Record of Intestate, 135
Sudan, 11, 109

INDEX

Survey for revenue purposes and records of rights, 4
Sweden, 15
Swiss Group, 60
Switzerland, 15
System of
  Conclusive title, 2
  Guaranteed Title, 2

T.G. Ashok Kumar vs. Govindammal & Others, 129
Thailand, 109
the English Group, 40
the German Group, 40
the Netherlands, 15, 35, 79
  Deed Registration, 33, 37
  Liability of Government for Loss to True Owner of Property, 35
  Registrar Plays Active Role, 36
  Notice to Parties before Entry into Cadastre, 36
  Registration Mandatory for Transfer of Title, 34
  Security of Title of a Bonafide Buyer, 35
  Single Agency for Deed Registration and Cadastre, 34
the Ottoman Group, 40
the Philippines, 15, 109
The Real Property Act, 1886, 54
the Swiss Group, 40
the Torrens Group, 40
Third Law Commission, 89
Tippan, 83
Title by Registration, 95
Title Registration, 2, 10
  Change-over to Not Advisable, 115
  Effect, 104
  Theory and Practice, 70
Title, Investigation of, 8
  Indexes to Facilitate Search, 9
Title, Registration Conclusive Proof of, 12
Torrens System, 2, 43, 49, 60

Torrens, Sir Robert Richard, 40, 42, 104
Transfer by Person other than Owner, 93, 138
Transfer Deed, Description of Property in the, 122
Transfer of immovable property, 136
Transfer of Part of Property, 125
Transfer of Property Act, 1882, 5, 76, 88, 130
Transfer of Property Act, Applicability of, 90
Transfer of Property, Conditional, 90, 137
Transfer of Property, History of Law, 88

Under the Land Registration Act, 2002, 54
United Kingdom (UK), 11, 15, 53
Untouchable and indestructible, 62
USA, 15, 18-27, 74, 80, 85-86, 97, 116-17
  Deed Registration, 18, 26
  Failed Experiment with Title Registration, 23
  History of Deed Registration, 19
  Marketable Title Acts, 21
  Order of Judicial Court for First Registration, 24
  Present Status of Title Registration, 23
  Title Insurance, 25
    Criticism of Title Insurance, 27
    Records Maintained by Insurance Agencies, 25
    Risk Elimination vs. Risk Assumption, 26
    Title Insurance makes up for Deficiencies in the System, 27
  Title, Investigation, 19
    Indexes Maintained by Registry, 20
Utility of Record-of-Rights, 81

Wadhwa, D.C., 2, 98, 102
Wales, 50, 53
Washington, 24
West Bengal, Record-of-Rights in, 159

Adjudication Procedures, 161
Administrative Machinery, 160
Coverage of Urban Area, 159
Legal Sanctity, 160
Preparation of Records, Cadastral Survey, Involvement of the Community, 160
Regular Updating of Records, 161

Role of Civil Courts, 161
Williams, Joshua, 89
Williams on Real Property, 89
World Bank, 86

Yugoslavia, 59

Zamindari system, 83